Project
Earth

Michael Dingle

Project Earth

Preserving the World God Created

WILLIAM B. BADKE

MULTNOMAH

Portland, Oregon

Unless otherwise indicated, all Scripture references are from the Holy Bible: New International Version, © 1973, 1978, 1984 by the International Bible Society. Used by permission of Zondervan Bible Publishers.

Cover illustration by Miles Pinkney
Edited by Rodney L. Morris

PROJECT EARTH
© 1991 by William B. Badke
Published by Multnomah Press
10209 SE Division Street
Portland, Oregon 97266

Multnomah Press is a ministry of Multnomah School of the Bible, 8435 NE Glisan Street, Portland, Oregon 97220.

Printed in the United States of America.

Library of Congress Cataloging-in-Publication Data
Badke, William G., 1949-
    Project earth : preserving the world God created / William B. Badke.
        p.   cm.
    Includes bibliographical references.
    ISBN 0-88070-423-6
    1. Human ecology—Religious aspects—Christianity. 2. Nature—Religious aspects—Christianity. 3. Earth. I. Title.
BT695.5.B33   1991
261.8'362—dc20   90-20207
                                                                              CIP

        90 91 92 93 94 95 96 97 98 99 - 10 9 8 7 6 5 4 3 2 1

Let all things their Creator bless,
And worship Him in humbleness,
O praise Him! Alleluia!

Contents

My neighbor liked to service his own car to save money. What could be easier than doing an oil change? Pull the plug, drain the oil, change the filter, reinsert the plug, and add new oil.

The only problem was that the container into which he deposited the dirty oil was a patch of gravel-covered ground. Every three months or so, he poured a gallon of sludge, full of contaminants, right into the soil.

About a hundred yards from his oil dump runs a stream which in turn winds through our small town. Just a few miles south, the land drops off sharply. This is not because nature made it so, but because the area attracts large gravel trucks which constantly pull out of our district full of pebbles and sand destined for new roads and parking lots.

I had a vision one day, though not the biblical kind. I imagined my neighbor's used oil leeching slowly, over the years, down to the stream. I saw it mixing its chemicals with the already less than pure creek water and skimming along the surface down to the gravel pits. From there, it spread deeper into the porous ground, eventually surfacing in the farms that cover the area to the east, at the bottom of the hill.

This was disturbing enough until I imagined a hundred million people all dumping their four gallons of sludge per year into the ground. Quick calculation made this four hundred million gallons of oil. I could not even conceive of such an amount.

Perhaps my daydream was just wild speculation, the product of watching too many episodes of "Nature" on public television. Who knows for sure how many people actually unburden used oil on the environment?

But I became puzzled by a small conflict that began in my mind—I cared, but I had no inclination to become committed. So unmoved was I that I wondered if even seeing all four hundred million gallons shimmering in a vast poisonous lake would have stirred me to action.

I never spoke to my neighbor about his troubling habit. He moved away and is probably polluting someone else's neighborhood. I did nothing about his problem, and I continued to say nothing about the mills and factories nearby which turn the skies varying shades of gray and brown.

There is an obvious excuse for my indifference. I am not an ecologist, nor the son of an ecologist. My adventure has been spiritual, in the realm of biblical studies and theology. The earth is nonspiritual, solid, concrete, part of all that we followers of Christ call transitory.

Evangelicals have not been overly active in the environmental debate. In fact, we have watched the rise of Greenpeace and Friends of the Earth with some dubiousness and even alarm. These organizations represent an extreme, a radicalism based on the false premise that the earth is the only environment humanity will ever have. We Christians know better, and look forward with expectancy to the day when we will leave this planet and be transported to a far more glorious heavenly existence.

To shift the metaphor, why should we devote time and energy to a sinking ship when the eternally golden shore is almost within our sight? Most of us have never been overly concerned with the temporal and merely physical, except, of course, when it relates to the health of our own bodies.

But now the environment's woes are encroaching on our space. It is scarcely possible to watch a half-hour news program without viewing at least one segment on pollution. Ecology is in our magazines and newspapers, in our politics. The environment is becoming more than a vaguely disturbing feature of our daily lives. Its plight, bombarded at us by the media, is having an effect on us, despite our desire to continue believing that the warning signals are only the premature rantings of radicals and freaks. All of a sudden, we are watching our cities scramble to find dump sites to replace our overburdened landfills, the maple trees of Canada die under the acid tumbling from the skies, and poisoned seals wash up by the thousands on European shores. We are beginning to believe that a crisis is emerging.

Why, if we evangelical Christians are to be salt and light to a lost and dying humanity, has it taken us so long to recognize that our physical environment is crumbling faster than the technicians can reassemble it? Why are we still wondering whether or not indifference will do as a response? We have certainly emotion enough for the abortion debate, pornography, and prayer in schools. Why are we more or less content to watch the world God made turn into a chemical swamp?

Surely the answer is to be found in our stress on the command of Christ: "Seek first the kingdom of God." All of the issues which genuinely provoke us have to do with *humanity* in its sin, *humanity* in its need for redemption. We have convinced ourselves that people issues are the only important concerns for the Christian. To defend the earth from destruction would be to divert our time and energy away from our God-given mandate to drag human beings out of the jaws of eternal destruction.

In our view, eternity counts. The earth, by comparison, does not. All that is temporal must be bypassed if we are to accomplish the task most needed—to win the world of humanity for Christ. If the physical creation is dying, that may be a matter for sorrow. But it is not a cause for the Christian to champion. The earth will one day perish anyway, but the eternal destiny of people rests on what they have done with Christ in this life.

This was once my justification for ignoring environmental concerns. There were simply too many other issues which have eternal ramifications. To get involved in ecology was to be "this worldly," to lose sight of the fact that "only what's done for Christ will last."

And then one day my tradition in theology and biblical studies brought me up short, face to face with the crumbling creation. I was preparing to teach a course on Jeremiah when Jeremiah 4:23-26 caught hold of me and has never let go. It reads:

> I looked at the earth,
>   and it was formless and empty;
> and at the heavens,
>   and their light was gone.
> I looked at the mountains,
>   and they were quaking;
> all the hills were swaying.
> I looked, and there were no people;
>   every bird in the sky had flown away.

I looked, and the fruitful land was a desert;
all its towns lay in ruins
before the LORD, before his fierce anger.

On the surface, this is a poetic image of Babylon's scorched earth policy used to put down rebellion. But the words that gripped me were "formless and empty," exactly the same terminology in the Hebrew as is found in Genesis 1:2 when describing the uncreated world. Could it be, I asked myself, that Jeremiah 4 is warning us of a potential uncreation, of the possibility that the physical world could unravel because of human sin?

Playing detective, I began to investigate further. To summarize what will take many pages to explain properly, I learned that the physical creation and what happens to it are profoundly theological, totally biblical concerns. I found that God cares about the world he has made and has allowed the environment to bear five distinct kinds of witness, each of which has ramifications for the way we present the gospel.

This book could have been titled: "How I Changed My Mind about the Environment." It is the work of someone who is a traditional, run-of-the-mill evangelical affirming the lordship of the risen Christ and the inerrancy of Scripture. Though neither a radical nor a particularly demonstrative crusader, I have become convinced that our evangelical silence about the destruction of God's creation must end, that believers must awaken to a new crisis and a new opportunity.

It may be possible, in responding biblically to this ever growing problem, that our very proclamation of the gospel will be empowered with a new dynamic. Such has usually been the case when humanity has been challenged by crisis. Each disaster which has befallen mankind has brought Christians a fresh means to announce the good news of Christ. Ironically, the very earth we have virtually ignored for so many centuries, may now in its own time of trauma become a means of announcing the Kingdom of God in a new way.

1

Creation in Crisis?

A letter in my possession is dated December 23, 1914. It reads:

Dear Gwen

Amy & Lily have sent me a delightful little present of mince pie, biscuits, and plum pudding. But now I've written to thank them I've forgotten their address. Would you please let them have this letter enclosed as soon as you can.

Hope you will all have a very good time this Christmas. I shall be thinking of you a lot of course. You know men's hearts go out to those at home this Christmas day.

Dear Daddy, Mother, Eva, Leonard, Ella, Chanley, Gwen, and Graham, a happy helpful Christmas to you all. I hope indeed Leonard in

Montreal will have a happy time.

In haste.

Your's affectionately
Will

The letterhead reads "Y.M.C.A. with H.M. Forces on Active Service."

This young man, whose plaintiveness comes out between the lines, was probably writing from a World War I battle area. If so, he had just lived through a period of fierce fighting. Yet the letter reveals a curious omission: There is not a single reference to the war.

The explanation may be a simple one. It is plain that young Will was preoccupied with thoughts of home and family on this day, two days before Christmas. Probably he was blocking out the conflagration around him and reflecting on memories of Christmases in better times. But it is still exceedingly strange that he had nothing to say about his current situation, especially in light of the seriousness of the dangers. Had he been warned off by the censors? Did he not want to worry his loved ones?

Evangelicals are committed to one central truth, that God, the King of the earth, has sent his Son to die for the sins of mankind and to rise again to bring salvation. This is the heart of our message, our consuming passion. As young Will longed for his family while he spent Christmas in the midst of horror, so we long for the souls around us so that they might share in the fellowship of Christ's loved ones. But Will said nothing about the crisis of his personal environment. Are we guilty of a similar omission?

Is it possible that our focus as evangelicals has narrowed to such an extent that some of the really important messages we need to convey are becoming muted? We have failed to speak adequately to the growing moral corruption in our society, instead relying upon gospel-transformed lives to cleanse the degradation. We often ignore the needs of the poor at our doorsteps, trusting that salvation will bring economic improvement.

And now we face this environmental problem. Though few of us can avoid hearing about it every day through some medium or other, it has not become an element in our proclamation of God's answer to a fallen world. Perhaps it does not need to be. The world is filled with crises of every kind, yet somehow human life goes on. We have, after all, an abundance of technicians to deal with the trauma in the physical creation. Somehow a solution will be found in due course, as solutions are found for most other ills in society.

This sort of thinking is not necessarily escapism. As Christians we know that we have only so much time and energy to meet the demands of the work God has called us to do. Thus we must set priorities, most of which appear to be far higher on the scale than ecological concern. Yet even as we ignore once again the dire warnings that our planet on its present course is perhaps only decades away from failing to sustain life, we must begin to wonder whether or not this crisis should have a higher priority.

Two questions become crucial and will form the basis of our discussion: *Is the danger to the environment severe enough to compel us to get involved? Can the ecological crisis reasonably be incorporated into our mission on earth as ambassadors of the saving God?*

HOW BAD IS THE SITUATION?

Are we being falsely bludgeoned by scare tactics or is there on the horizon a global crisis which will compel our involvement?

In 1982, Dr. Milo Don Appleman published his book *Epitaph for Planet Earth: How to Survive the Approaching End of the Human Species.*[1] The preface to this work on the ravages of pollution and resource depletion begins: "You may find the facts related in this book to be frightening. Good. You should be scared."

Dr. Appleman is not a quack nor a scare-monger. He is professor emeritus and former head of the department of bacteriology at the University of Southern California. He is listed in *Who's Who in the World, Who's Who in Science from Antiquity to Present,* and *Outstanding Educators of America. Encyclopedia Britannica* has used him as a contributor.

Here we have as solid a citizen in the scientific community as one could hope to find. And this man is predicting the demise of all humanity unless the earth's ecological trauma is quickly alleviated.

Should we be scared? Let's consider some of the evidence.

Toxic Waste

In 1953 the Niagara Falls Board of Education bought land which consisted of a filled in canal owned by Occidental Petroleum's Hooker Chemical and Plastics Corporation. Homes were built on the ten-block site, as well as an elementary school and playing fields.

During the years that followed, there were vague suspicions that the health problems of the residents—eye and skin irritations, stomach disorders, miscarriages, birth defects, cancers, and so on—were more prevalent than was the norm for other areas.

But it was not until 1977 that a flood from the nearby Niagara River began washing the culprit into the area's basements—an odorous sludge containing benzene, trichloroethylene, and dioxin. Investigation determined that Hooker Chemical, between 1942 and 1953, had dumped 21,800 tons of chemical waste into the canal, named after William Love, a former owner. They had then filled in the waterway before turning the land over for residential development.

Today, the area is once again being resettled, but the federal government is several million dollars poorer due to the cost of relocating the former residents and capping the site. Even more seriously, the former occupants of the Love Canal development face an uncertain future, with probable high risks of cancer and other diseases in the coming years.[2]

If this were an isolated incident, we might simply shudder and then get on with our lives. But none of us knows when Love Canal might happen in our neighborhood. The U.S. Environmental Protection Agency (EPA) lists 25,089 potentially hazardous waste sites in the United States alone.[3] There are many also in Canada and Europe. Even more serious are the number of unknown sites which could surprise almost anyone of us by bursting their containers and leaking into our lives.

One of the biggest dangers of such waste is the contamination of the ground water which supplies wells, rivers, and lakes. An EPA test of a thousand wells in 1986 found 23 percent of them to be contaminated by organic-chemical substances. Of the more than sixty-five thousand chemicals now being used in American agriculture and industry, a good number are finding their way into drinking water, resulting in a reported 85,875 water-borne illnesses from 1971 to 1988.[4] No one knows how many were not reported.

Any number of toxic materials horror stories abound: The December 1984 leak of deadly pesticide in Bhopal,

India, which killed twenty-five hundred people and permanently maimed seventeen thousand; the November 1986 dump of toxic substances into the Rhine River in Germany, which wiped out hundreds of thousands of fish and eels; the June 1988 revelation that the supposedly safe chemical storage area rented by an Italian businessman in Koko, Nigeria, contained eight thousand barrels, many of them leaking deadly PCBs (polychlorinated biphenyls, linked with cancers, liver diseases, birth defects, and spontaneous abortions).

This latter example reveals another difficulty. Though our industries are producing an ever increasing number of dangerous chemical by-products, we lack sufficient means to dispose of them safely. Thus there are increasing efforts by some of the more unscrupulous waste disposal companies to dump these hazardous products on third world nations.

All of this does not begin to touch the most potentially serious problem of all—the treatment of radioactive substances, which do not lose their deadly properties for hundreds of years. The nuclear reactor disaster at Chernobyl has only emphasized the fears of many that a proliferation of nuclear power stations is flirting with catastrophe.

Air Pollution

Most of us who live in or near major cities are well acquainted with smog, that brown pall which hovers overhead, encapsulating us, and at times attacking our eyes, throat, and lungs. As someone who has long been plagued with allergies and lung problems, it took a move thirty-four miles out of Vancouver, British Columbia, to be sure of escaping the smog zone. And Vancouver is not a heavy pollution area.

We often blame industry, though automobile emissions contribute more to the problem. But there could be a case made for seeing air pollution as a natural phenomenon. Noel Grove writes:

> Decay, sea spray, and volcanic eruptions annually release more sulfur than all the power plants, smelters, and other industries in the world. Lightning bolts create nitrogen oxides just as automobiles and industrial furnaces do, and trees emit hydrocarbons called terpenes. Their release triggers a bluish haze that gave the Blue Ridge its name.[5]

Before we blame our problems on nature, however, we must recognize that the earth is fully equipped to neutralize only natural pollutants. When we throw our additional chemicals into the air, we are putting the natural neutralizing systems into crisis. In North America, we may not have reached the air pollution level of a Cubatao, Brazil (where attempts to breathe can on some days bring vomiting and the rain is so acidic that it burns the skin) or Mexico City (whose residents breathe toxins equivalent to smoking two packs of cigarettes per day). But our situation is bad enough.

Denver, Colorado, has had such a severe problem with winter carbon dioxide and smog levels that strict restrictions have been put on both automobile and industrial fuels. Los Angeles is well known for its intense smogs which periodically force people with breathing problems to stay indoors. Even Toronto, Canada, in summer 1988 was so laden with air pollution that serious health hazards were experienced.

The worst difficulties with air pollution, however, may not be the ones we see and smell. The chemicals we have poured into the skies are rising into the upper atmosphere where they are able to do damage of global proportions.

Acid Rain. While acid rain has become a worldwide problem, for North America the most seriously affected area is eastern Canada. Smelter, power plant, and motor vehicle emissions, primarily from the northeastern United States, combine with rain drops, making a chemically acidic liquid which is disseminated on Canada's forests and lakes with every storm. In eastern Canada, some fourteen thousand lakes are either dead or dying because animal life cannot survive in the increased acidity of their waters. The same is true of a number of more acid sensitive forms of plant life.

Two symbols of Canada tell the tale: The maple trees, from which the Canadian national emblem—the maple leaf—is derived, are dying in the millions. In Ottawa, the form of a woman representing Canada is carved into the base of a statue. The woman's cheeks have vertical acid rain lines etched into them, as if she were weeping.[6]

The Ozone Layer. In the lower stratosphere is a layer of oxygen which has been bombarded by ultraviolet rays from the sun. The resulting gas, known as ozone, is able to absorb much of the sun's radiation.

In 1983, scientists involved in the British Antarctic survey discovered that the concentration of ozone in the stratosphere above Antarctica was markedly depleted. A 1987 American study costing ten million dollars confirmed that there was indeed a "hole" in the ozone layer. Now there are signs that a similar ozone depletion is beginning in the arctic as well.

Several substances are capable of destroying ozone faster than it can rebuild itself. Some, like methane and nitrous oxide, are produced by natural phenomena, such as decay of vegetation. But we have added mightily to the nitrous oxide problem by burning fossil fuels. Even more dangerous to ozone are the man-made chlorofluorocarbons, used in refrigeration units, aerosol cans, and some styrofoams. Once in a gaseous form, these substances work havoc on ozone, and are its greatest enemy.

What will happen if ozone levels drop even lower? Medical specialists warn of increased sunburns, skin cancers, cataracts, and breakdown in human immune systems. Agriculturalists fear decreasing crop yield. The severe sunburns among members of arctic expeditions in the winter of 1988 may be the first real evidence of what is to come.

The Greenhouse Effect. The same process by which pollutants move into the upper atmosphere to destroy ozone is also at work in what may be the greatest modern threat to our planet—the warming of the earth. Here we are working with scientific models rather than a great deal of hard evidence, but the principle is simple enough.

Since the mid-1800s, the level of carbon dioxide in the atmosphere has increased by 27 percent.[7] The main source is the burning of fossil fuels, a practice which has decreased in the western world, but is increasing rapidly in the Third World. Beyond this, the enormous loss of rain forests in this century has severely limited the amount of vegetation which can be used to absorb carbon dioxide.[8]

Carbon dioxide acts very much like the glass of a greenhouse. It allows heat from the sun to be absorbed by the earth but then prevents the heat from escaping into the upper atmosphere. If carbon dioxide increases, so too does its ability to hold in heat. Then its good properties become a problem because it traps too much heat in the lower atmosphere. With the currently rising levels of this gas, scientists predict that the earth's median temperature will go up within the next sixty years by 2.5 to 7.5 degrees Fahrenheit.

What this will produce is open to a good deal of speculation, but reputable climatologists have spoken of widespread droughts, melting of polar ice, and massive flooding of coastal areas. The very regions which are now the bread baskets of the world may become perpetual wastelands where famine is the norm.

While the mechanism of the greenhouse effect is simple, recent studies are showing that the results may be complex. It appears that the world's climate functions in ways not obvious even to the experts. Thus, while most scientists predict global warming, others are arguing that changes in ocean currents and increased evaporation over land masses may do just the opposite and trigger a cooling trend.

In any case, the greenhouse effect, brought about by man-made carbon dioxides, is likely to bring catastrophic changes in human life. Perhaps it has already begun: the very severe drought conditions in central North America in summer 1988 are being held up by some scientists as evidence that we may not have to wait sixty years to experience the global disaster they are predicting.

Recently the debate over the greenhouse effect has become even more muddled. Some scientists are now scoffing at the notion of its existence; others have cut in half their predictions of temperature increases. But many continue to hold fast to their original warnings. Regardless of our views on the issue, it remains the height of foolishness to ignore the problem, just in case it does not happen.

The Rain Forests

Over eleven million hectares of tropical rain forest are destroyed annually. In thirty years this will amount to an area the size of India. The forests are being cleared primarily for agriculture and urban development. In Brazil, for example, large areas of existing agricultural land have long been held by a few landowners. In order to allow young families to develop farms in the absence of available land, the Brazilian government has declared open season on the rain forest.

We have already seen that rain forest depletion is a factor in the increase of carbon dioxide in the atmosphere. But many other serious problems have become apparent.

Brazil, in particular, provides a model for the results of forest depletion. In order to prepare the land rapidly for planting, the new settlers have been burning the trees and undergrowth of the rain forest. This burning alone accounts for 10 percent of the world's production of carbon dioxide. In the past few years thousands of square miles of Brazilian rain forest have gone up in smoke.[9]

As the farmers clear their land, the tribal peoples who lived in the area have been beaten back into an ever shrinking jungle, and they are dying by the thousands, primarily from diseases once unknown to them, but occasionally as the result of violent clashes with the new settlers.[10] Dying too are species of plants and animals which exist nowhere else. This is even more serious when we recognize that well over half of all the species on earth live in rain forests. At the present rate of deforestation, there will be no rain forests left by the year 2135, according to conservative estimates. Less conservative projections give the forests less than one hundred years.[11] In the process, thousands of varieties of living things will simply cease to exist.

The new president of Brazil, Fernando Collor de Mello, has reversed his country's policy on rain forest development. We can only hope that he is not too late.

The real irony is that rain forest land, after two or three years, can support neither crops nor cattle. The forest acts like a giant sponge to soak up and hold moisture. When it is removed, not only does the land lose its source of organic nutrients, but it cannot hold water, rainfall decreases, and weeds spread rapidly.[12] The result is a further step: desertification, by which usable land becomes barren desert. This has already occurred in the Andes Mountains, the Himalayas, and East Africa. While the Amazon may fare better under proper conservation measures, the haste of its settlement spells serious danger.

With deforestation comes increased risk of floods and landslides. Several recent such "natural" disasters were not really natural at all. They occurred because vital vegetation which could have held back the mud and water had been removed.

Agricultural Land

I used to live in South Burnaby, British Columbia, right next to Vancouver. Across the street from our home were several "urban gardens," small acreages which produce large quantities of vegetables. The December 16, 1988 issue of the *Vancouver Sun* newspaper released the shocking news that vegetables from a number of these urban gardens, vegetables I have eaten, were contaminated with a dangerous heavy metal called cadmium.

That hits pretty close to home, but it is not surprising. Toxic waste has a way of spreading its influence through the soil. This small example, however, is of little consequence in comparison with the ecological woes facing agriculture today. Our intensive farming practices, especially since World War II, have brought us salinization and alkalinization of the irrigated ground, nitrate pollution of ground waters, and pesticide residues in our food.[13] Our soil is being depleted of nutrients so that it takes more and more chemical fertilizer to produce the same yield.

On our prairies, the natural grasses have been replaced by grain crops. During the months of the year when there is only stubble on the ground, the winds carry the topsoil away. Without the prairie grass, there is little to hold it in place. For many years now, the loss of agricultural topsoil in North America has greatly outstripped its replenishment by the processes of decay.

The list of ecological crises could go on. We have not even begun to discuss the pollution of our oceans,[14] the compounding problems of the population explosion, and the ever-present danger of a nuclear winter brought about by global war. The plain and simple reality is that we are destroying our environment. At the present rate of pollution growth, the earth could be largely uninhabitable within a hundred years, according to the many world delegates to an environmental conference held in the summer of 1988.[15]

Is there reason to be frightened? Yes, there is. In January 1989, *Time* magazine did not have a "man (or woman) of the year." Instead, it named a "Planet of the Year: Endangered Earth." The editors pointed out that the ecological crisis had been the number one news story of 1988. Was it a coincidence that *National Geographic* only a month before had devoted its December issue to "Endangered Earth"?

IS IT TIME FOR CHRISTIANS TO BECOME INVOLVED?

Here, instantly, we show our habitual hesitation. The ecological problem requires technology which is beyond most of us. Should it not be left to the technicians? Is there really any room for us to bring in some sort of Christian view of ecology?

Before we too hastily pass the problem along to others, we need to be aware that a sizable number of ecologists already view Christians as deeply involved in the crisis— but on the wrong side, as the *source* of the trouble in the environment.

In the late sixties, historian Lynn White published an article which may well be the most cited work in all of the ecological debate. White argued that the Judeo-Christian heritage, with its rejection of the worship of nature and its biblical mandate for man to have dominion over the earth, was the driving force behind the western world's abuse of the environment.[16] According to White, "Christianity, in absolute contrast to ancient paganism and Asia's religions . . . not only established a dualism of man and nature, but also insisted that it is God's will that man exploit nature for his proper ends."[17]

Even more harsh was an article by Jackson Lee Ice, published in 1975. Ice, then a professor of religion at Florida State University, argued among other things that followers of Christ have never cared a great deal about the physical world because they see it as doomed.[18] He parodied the Christian view as follows:

> By the end of the age the world, condemned by God since the Fall like an old tenement house, will be worn and used up, so why bother with its care? Earth is merely a stopping place, a testing ground, a shadowy vale of tears, a material stepping-stone to a higher spiritual realm, or a disposable mechanical asteroid.[19]

The charges by White, Ice, and the many other ecologists riding on their bandwagon appear to be serious.

Fortunately, perhaps, for us, biblical scholars have been hard at work shooting the bandwagon full of holes.

The ecological critics of the Christian tradition have missed a number of vital facts: that God's command was to *tend* the garden, not to exploit it; that God never gave human beings absolute power to do what they wanted; that God himself modeled a pattern for environmental care which would please even the most jaded ecologist (see Job 38-39; Psalm 104); that modern science was born essentially out of a *rejection* of Christian values; that societies with no Judeo-Christian tradition also abuse nature; and that cultural motives such as the North American frontier mentality, were probably more influential than religious values in creating our present crisis.[20]

Even if we can dismiss Lynn White, however, an uneasiness remains because we recognize that Christianity throughout history has had a relationship with nature which, to use H. Paul Santmire's terminology, has been "ambiguous."[21] It is here, perhaps, where our greatest failure lies.

We are guilty, not of the sin of commission (an ethic which drove the West into exploitation of the environment), but of omission. Earlier, two important questions were raised: Is the ecological situation so serious that Christians must be involved? And is there a way in which the ecological crisis can be incorporated into God's mandate for Christians on earth? Taking into account that the ecological trauma is serious enough to cause us to fear for human survival, it would seem that all people, including Christians, should be involved in a solution. But we have done virtually nothing. Why? *The second question keeps getting in the way of the first.*

Christians are unique in that they have an overriding mission for Christ. We who follow our Lord consider ourselves to be his ambassadors at his bidding. We tend to shy away from the trappings of this temporal world. We do not want to be side-tracked.

We have convinced ourselves that the earthly realm is not part of the heavenly call. No matter how serious the crisis may be, we will not be moved to act unless we are sure it falls within the divine mandate. Until we can be sure that God intends Christians to be involved in solving the plight of the earth, we will leave the problem to others. Thus the very devotion to our Lord which has made Christians the envy and the scorn of history, is now holding us back from getting involved in the impending doom of our physical environment.

But what if the nonhuman creation were found to be significant both to God and to his program? What if our fear of the entrapment of the physical had been overly influenced by a misinterpretation of Scripture? Would it make a difference?

The current environmental movement is crying out for a basic philosophy to guide it. Lewis Moncrief has argued that three obstacles stand in the way of modern man beating the ecological crisis: "(I) an absence of personal moral direction concerning our treatment of our natural resources, (II) an inability on the part of our social institutions to make adjustments to this stress, and (III) an abiding faith in technology."[22]

There is no value in trying to convince society to get to work to solve the problem and in relying on technology as a cure-all if there is no moral will to give people a reason and commitment to act. Christianity has long championed itself as the moral answer to man's ills. Is it possible that a new look at the Scriptures could convince us that ecology should now be placed on the Christian agenda? Could it be part of our mission? If it could, we would be in a unique position to provide society with a rationale to address the trauma in the physical creation.

Even if society refused to listen to us, such a biblical and theological reassessment of God's view of nature should reveal to us the truth which I believe is in total harmony with Scripture: *This is our Father's world, and we Christians must end our sinful indifference to its plight.*

Notes

1. Milo Don Appleman, *Epitaph for Planet Earth: How to Survive the Approaching End of the Human Species* (New York: Frederick Fell Publishers, 1982).

2. Melanie L. Griffin, "The Legacy of Love Canal," *Sierra*, January/February 1986, 26-28.

3. Eleanor Smith, "Angry Housewives," *Omni*, December 1986, 113.

4. Rich Levine, "Watergate," *Omni*, February 1988, 20.

5. Noel Grove, "Air: An Atmosphere of Uncertainty," *National Geographic*, April 1987, 512.

6. Jo Currie, "Who'll Stop the Acid Rain?" *Canadian Living*, 1 October 1988, 111-13. See also Mark Mardon, "Canada's View on Acid Rain," *Sierra*, July/August 1987, 20-22.

7. Grove, 518.

8. See Kenneth E. F. Watt, s.v. "Environment," *Encyclopedia Britannica 1987 Yearbook of Science and the Future*.

9. See Marguerite Johnson, "The Amazon Goes Up in Flames," *Time*, 12 September 1988, 74.

10. For an update on Brazil's deforestation and its relation to tribal extinction, see William S. Ellis, "Rondonia's Settlers Invade Brazil's Imperiled Rain Forest," and Loren McIntyre, "Last Days of Eden: Rondonia's Urueu-Wau-Wau Indians," *National Geographic*, December 1988, 772-99, 801-17.

11. Kenneth E. F. Watt, s.v. "Environment," *Encyclopedia Britannica 1988 Yearbook of Science and the Future*. For less conservative estimates see

Donald R. Perry, "The Canopy of the Tropical Rain Forest," *Scientific American*, November 1984, 146-47.

12. Peter Alleshire, "Betwitched," *Omni*, January 1988, 22.

13. *Our Common Future: World Commission on the Environment and Development* (New York: Oxford University Press, 1987), 58.

14. See Anastasia Toufexis, "The Dirty Seas," *Time*, 1 August 1988, 40-46.

15. Toronto, Canada: "The Changing Atmosphere's Implications for Global Security." See Russell Felton, "No Time to Waste," *The Review*, 72 (Winter 1988): 10-15.

16. Lynn White, "The Historical Roots of our Ecologic Crisis," *Science*, 155 (March 1967): 1203-7; reprinted in *The Environmental Handbook*, ed. Garrett de Bell (New York: Ballantine Books, 1970), 12-26, and in many other environmental collections. White was not actually the first to propose this argument. See the work of the Zen Buddhist D. T. Suzuki, "The Role of Nature in Zen Buddhism," in *Zen Buddhism: Selected Writings of D. T. Suzuki*, ed. William Barrett (Garden City, N.Y.: Doubleday, 1956), 229-58.

17. White, "Historical Roots" in *Environmental Handbook*, 20.

18. Jackson Lee Ice, "The Ecological Crisis: Radical Monotheism vs. Ethical Pantheism," *Religion in Life*, 44 (1975): 203-11.

19. Ibid., 205.

20. See especially the articles collected in *Ecology and Religion in History*, ed. David and Eileen Spring (New York: Harper & Row, 1974); and George S. Hendry, *Theology of Nature* (Philadelphia: Westminster Press, 1980), 172, 197.

21. H. Paul Santmire, *The Travail of Nature: The Ambiguous Ecological Promise of Christian Theology* (Philadelphia: Fortress Press, 1985).

22. Lewis W. Moncrief, "The Cultural Basis for our Environmental Crisis," *Ecology and Religion in History*, 85.

2

Creation as Witness

We had heard rumors of a waterfall to the west of Rolley Lake, but my son Shawn and I had never searched for it on our regular rambles in the area. The day we set out to find it, neither of us expected very much. The stream which ran out of the lake was shallow and flowed slowly. No waterfall was marked on our map.

Following the stream, we noticed faint signs of others who had also taken up the quest. But there were no real paths to follow. As we went, the land began to slope downward. The water running beside us picked up its tempo. This was at least grounds for some expectancy.

Then suddenly it was there. The whole earth fell away in front of us, and a wild torrent of water (where had it all come from?) plunged a hundred feet down into nowhere. It roared and twisted, foam-white, cutting deeply through rock and over the cliff. This was not nature in its bouncy and delightful mode. This was gut-wrenching nature that turned my son and I instantly into minuscule specks on an infinite landscape. This was nature that made you shudder with its power. You wanted to cut yourself off from it for fear of being dragged down into its roaring energy, to certain extinction. Beautiful, yes. But the beauty of awe and fear that put you firmly in your place.

Descending the slope, we found that darkness was coming rather faster than we had anticipated. We had scarcely more than a few minutes to look down upon the deep pool at the bottom, which seemed capable of absorbing any amount of cascading water. Then we went home.

Were we different for our discovery? I believe so, just as each of us is changed and shaped by similar rare encounters with creation unchained. At times it is difficult to articulate the experience, but it has something to do with a recognition that we are not the masters of all we survey, that we are not the captains of our fate.

In essence, it is an encounter with God. No, nature is not itself divine. We know that. But nature serves as a *witness* to God, to make him apparent to the world through two particular testimonies which we may label "glory" and "nurture."

In those moments when we are brought up short by creation's beauty or power or terrifying awesomeness, the witness is particularly significant. It tells us that the God who made the world cannot be locked into the box of our human routines, of our mundane expectancies. It tells us that the Maker is truly the Maker, the one who both created the idea of all that is, and its realization.

If we are to formulate a biblical response to the ecological crisis, we must begin here, with creation at its most primal. We must begin with God's original view of the world he formed from nothing.

THE MEANING OF CREATION'S GOODNESS

The first divine evaluation of the universe God made is recorded in several places in Genesis 1—"God saw that it was good." This simple repeated statement acts like a refrain, almost poetic in form, announcing the Creator's pleasure in the world he designed and built.

We generally assume that we understand the meaning of the evaluation. Good is good. It is everything that is not bad. But we must remember what we are considering here. We are viewing an earth untouched by anyone but God. We are seeing it as he made it. What is "good" in that context? Is it "beautiful" or "right" or "perfect" or just what?

Perhaps an exact definition may not seem important, but it is vital to our understanding of the meaning of our present crisis. If we could grasp the original design, if we could see what God saw on the day he rested from all he had made and watched it with unbounded joy, perhaps it would speak volumes to us by way of contrast with the world we inherited. Obviously we human beings have done things to the earth which are making it incapable of supporting life as it did. If we are to find a biblical way back, we must begin with a clear view of creation as it was when it was new, so that we can see its present state in the proper light.

What is the meaning of God's declaration that creation was "good"? First, it was *built according to plan.* This is basic. Genesis 1 elucidates the important doctrine of *creation ex nihilo,* creation out of nothing, out of the mere speaking of the Creator. God said . . . and it was so. If creation's goodness means nothing else, it surely describes that God's blueprint was fully and in every detail brought to life in the physical reality. What God made was what he planned to make.

Ancient Gnosticism, the church's second serious heresy (after the Judaizers), sought to deny this crucial truth by arguing that God formed the earth through intermediaries so that he could not be touched by or blamed for the innate sinfulness of physical matter. But nothing of this is seen in the creation account. God planned the world and he made it and he is responsible for it because it is his, built exactly to plan.

Second, creation was *orderly*. The Old Testament abounds with a type of literature which biblical scholars call "Wisdom." This genre is rooted in human experience, teaching the life skills by which a man or woman may operate successfully under God's dominion. Examples include Job, Proverbs, Ecclesiastes, Song of Solomon, as well as a number of Psalms.

It is particularly the Wisdom Literature of Scripture that stresses creation's goodness because of its order, but the concept is found throughout the Bible. Genesis 1 is built upon a rigid structure involving cycles of repeated patterns. The effect is boldly to proclaim that the creation itself was shaped within the rigors of an unremitting order. Isaiah 45:18 announces: "He did not create it to be empty [the word from Genesis 1:1 depicting the barren waste before God gave it shape], but formed it to be inhabited." In other words, God did not create a homogeneous, undetailed clump of mud, but a world of distinctions, of inhabitants, of diversity, and thus of order by which it is so beautifully organized.

There is a growing consensus among many Old Testament theologians that Wisdom Literature is based on the fact that the world is created by God and thus has order. The heart of Wisdom is the recognition that there is a meaning to all experience, a meaning founded on the premise that the world, made by God, is orderly, structured, with "an overarching harmony."[1]

To ask a biblical Wisdom writer what it means for creation to be "good" would immediately elicit the response: "It has order." Creation is structured by the God who structures all life. Because the physical world is ordered perfectly by the Maker, we may understand that human experience has the same sort of underlying order to it.

This is nowhere better seen than in the wisdom book of Job. After Job and his four friends have struggled hopelessly for the meaning of the seeming chaos which is human life, God responds with a nature lesson. In Job 38-41, God details the way in which he ordered his creation so that everything works just as he planned it. His implication is obvious: The God whose wisdom formed an ordered world is the God who has ordered human experience. No matter how chaotic life may seem, true wisdom understands that God is in full control. J. A. Loader writes, "The existence of the world means: not chaos, but order. And if humans wish to exist in this order, they should integrate into the creational order. This is what wisdom is all about."[2]

Finally, creation was *responsive*. The goodness of creation means more than a correspondence to God's plan and an integral order. There is also a vitality to the world God made, because God is the source of its life. Creation has a relationship with God in which it responds to him as Maker, acknowledging his power and grace.

A number of passages show the earth singing to God (Psalm 96:1, 11-13; 97:1). Psalm 148:3-6 declares:

> Praise him, sun and moon,
>> praise him, all you shining stars.
> Praise him, you highest heavens
>> and you waters above the skies.

Let them praise the name of the LORD,
  for he commanded and they were created.
He set them in place for ever and ever;
  he gave a decree that will never pass away.

We might dismiss this element as mere poetic license, but it embodies a basic and vital truth: all that exists is created to acknowledge the God who made it. Nothing lives for its own praise. It gives its praise to God. For creation to be good, it must be responsive in worship before God. If it is not, then it exists for itself and thus denies the Maker. Then it ceases to be good.

CREATION'S WITNESS TO GOD

First Witness: Glory

Creation bears witness to God in at least five ways. The first of these witnesses is nature's testimony to *the glory of the Creator*. This first witness is primary because there is nothing more basic to existence than the glorification of God. Quite simply, as Psalm 19:1 announces,

The heavens declare the glory of God;
  the skies proclaim the work of his hands.

Viewed with eyes that see beyond the mere givenness of the created order, the world God made speaks immense volumes about the complexity, greatness, and wondrous power of the Creator. That is why, standing before an unexpected waterfall, or coming upon a deer in the woods, one feels the urge to worship. Nature constantly points us beyond itself, saying, "See! See the One who made all this." As Robert Meye has put it, "To contemplate nature is an invitation to wonder."[3]

For many, this declaration of the glory of God, this invitation to wonder, is ignored altogether. They walk almost blindly in this world, guided only by the tunnel-vision of their personal concerns. For such people, there are no glorious sunsets or moments to stop and smell the roses.

But this in no way negates the validity of the witness. God's creation in its amazing inter-connected complexity acknowledges the Maker who is greater than anything he has made. Take a flower. Pull it apart. View the pieces under a magnifying glass, under a microscope. Something as insignificant as a tulip or a daisy encompasses a world of detail which could keep us studying it for the rest of our lives.

Nothing that lives, nothing that moves and grows, is outside of the majesty of this great wonder—that it was all made by God.

How could this magnificent world have come to be unless Someone, of an intellect beyond anything we can imagine, designed it? The facile explanation that all of this evolved should never be able to satisfy those who are truly using the minds God has given them. The very language of evolution reveals its self-doubts as it speaks of a seemingly purposeful natural selection process bringing about just those features needed by each species. Who knew these features were needed? How did the work of mutation, which almost always weakens a species, create the majesty we see in the life forms of earth?

All of this, of course, is very much beside the point. We believers are not showing a mindless gullibility when we affirm that God made the world. Romans 1:18-20 strongly affirms that nature's witness to God's glory is very much alive:

> The wrath of God is being revealed from heaven against all the godlessness and wickedness of men who suppress the truth by their wickedness,

> since what may be known about God is plain to
> them, because God has made it plain to them.
> For since the creation of the world God's invisi-
> ble qualities—his eternal power and divine
> nature—have been clearly seen, being under-
> stood from what has been made, so that men are
> without excuse.

No human being can observe the creation without
knowing that there is a Creator. If we choose to deny it,
that is a different matter. But we all begin with a recognition of God, for all of us have seen or heard creation's testimony to his glory.

Two examples will suffice to show the folly of denying
earth's origin in God. Julian Huxley, the eminent scientist
and evolutionist, in his book *Evolution in Action*, explains
that the odds against a horse having evolved by chance
alone was one thousand to the millionth power. It would
take three large volumes of five hundred pages each to
print a number like that. Huxley comments:

> No one would bet on anything so improbable
> happening; and yet it *has* happened. It has hap-
> pened, thanks to the workings of natural selec-
> tion and the properties of living substance which
> make natural selection inevitable.[4]

One only has to stand in amazement at the depth of
Huxley's faith in his replacement god: natural selection.

The naturalist Konrad Lorenz, in his fascinating book
On Aggression, took a similar direction. After detailing the
almost unbelievable complexity of animal instinctual
behavior, he presented the case for evolution:

> Natural causal associations always turn out to be
> grander and more awe-inspiring than even the
> most imaginative mythical explanation. The true

scientist does not need the inexplorable, the supernatural, to evoke his reverence: for him there is only one miracle, namely, that everything, even the finest flowerings of life, have come into being without miracles; for him the universe would lose some of its grandeur if he thought that any phenomenon . . . could be accounted for only by an *infringement* of the omnipresent and omnipotent laws of *one* universe.[5]

Having abandoned the true Creator of all things, the scientist is to make the process of evolution his omnipotent god. Seemingly for Lorenz, the more unlikely an explanation, the more it embodies the miraculous. One has to wonder where the sharp reasoning powers of science have gone in this flight of fancy.

The witness of creation cannot be denied. If it is true that it is the fool who says in his heart that there is no God, it is equally true that only the fool can look at creation and believe that it all fell into place by blind chance.

Thus, in the created world, we have a testimony which must be viewed as part of God's common grace—the special benefit that falls on all people, regardless of their association (or lack of it) with God. Creation bears witness that all that is here, including human life, originates from the glorious God to whom we are all responsible.

In its planning, its order, and its responsiveness to the Maker, creation tells us that we are not alone, isolated without explanation. We are not accidental but made, formed for purposes beyond our own abilities to decide and act. If we deny this testimony, we must do so against all the evidence. If we accept the truth of creation's witness to God's glory, our deepest questions will ultimately find their answers.

Second Witness: Nurture

When God had completed the creation of the world, he announced that the green plants would be food, not just for mankind but for all the animals as well (Genesis 1:29-30). Obviously, if he made human and animal life with a built-in need for daily nourishment, he would have had to provide the means for that nourishment.

But God's goodness moved beyond mere sustenance. He became the very Source of the ongoing life of all things. We must see Eden as the perfect ecosystem, where the existence of every organism helped to guarantee the ongoing existence of every other organism. Above it all was the nurturing God. Fertility was everywhere, abundant and unending, for the Maker had provided every means for life to be full in every respect. The description of the Garden in Genesis 2:4-14 gives no hint of any lack. Instead, all of creation bore witness, not just to God's glory but to his power to nurture life, to sustain richly the life forms he had made.

We find this power of nurture in many passages of Scripture. God asks in Job 38:25-28:

> "Who cuts a channel for the torrents of rain,
>   and a path for the thunderstorm,
> to water a land where no man lives,
>   a desert with no one in it,
> to satisfy a desolate wasteland
>   and make it sprout with grass?
> Does the rain have a father?
>   Who fathers the drops of dew?"

The fascinating nature Psalm, 104, after describing the incredible interaction of all created things, turns to a prayer which epitomizes the nurturing work of God:

These all look to you
   to give them their food at the proper time.
When you give it to them,
   they gather it up;
when you open your hand,
   they are satisfied with good things.
When you hide your face,
   they are terrified;
when you take away their breath,
   they die and return to the dust.
When you send your Spirit,
   they are created,
   and you renew the face of the earth. (vv. 27-
30; cf. Psalm 145:15-16; 147:7-18; Matthew 6:26)

The first witness—glory—called for worship. The second witness—nurture—demands a recognition of our utter dependence on the Maker. As we look at our environment, as we realize how much we need the plants and the air and the water and the animals for our survival, creation in turn points to God for *its* survival. Nature announces that God made this world to nurture us. Without his ongoing sustaining work, life would cease. It would take nothing more than a sustained drought or a flood or a cold snap when it should be warm, and God could turn our self-sufficiency on its head. We need him, for he controls our existence. By his nurturing presence, we continue to live.

As with the first witness, the witness of nurture is denied by many in our world. They see the earth as a closed system, self-generated and governed by its own laws. But this does not negate the testimony. For those who truly look, the evidence is there. God has provided, and continues to provide, all the means for the nurture of what he created.

ENHANCING THE WITNESS

In a creation which extols the glory and nurturing power of God, the Creator has made a special creature, the only one formed in God's image. For man, there was a special mandate not given to any other creature: *work the garden* (Genesis 2:15).

To understand our mandate as human beings, we must begin with the concept of "image." For centuries, most biblical scholars interpreted man's creation in the image of God with a focus on man's being: his personality and his moral similarities which allow him to communicate with the Creator and obey his will.

In more recent times, however, fresh study of the biblical concept of image has led scholars in another direction. It is now argued that image refers less to *being* than to *function* as the representatives of God. Consider Genesis 1:26. Having declared that he will create man in his image, God commands:

> "And let them rule over the fish of the sea and
> the birds of the air, over the livestock, over all
> the earth, and over all the creatures that move
> along the ground."

The whole statement—the call to make man in his image and the dominion command—is expressed in one sentence, as if the very meaning of being formed in God's image is to have rule over the earth as God has rule. Is there other evidence to support this understanding of image?

Yes, there is. Archaeology has revealed a common feature of ancient Near Eastern life: a king who could not visit every part of his realm regularly had images of himself placed everywhere. These images *represented* his rule locally, reminding the king's subjects where their true allegiance lay. To speak of an image in this context was immediately to evoke the concept of representation.[6]

A further indication comes from Genesis 9:6,

> "Whoever sheds the blood of man,
> by man shall his blood be shed;
> for in the image of God
> has God made man."

If "image" embodies the idea of representing God (ruling as God rules), then this verse makes ample sense—to slay a man is to attack God, for human beings represent God in his rule on earth. The murderer has committed the ultimate sin and loses his own life at the hands of God's representatives.[7]

William Dyrness has made an interesting parallel between *image* as a mandate to represent God on earth, and the Lord's mandate to the kings of Israel. These kings did not rule absolutely but as servants representing God, who was the actual sovereign (Deuteronomy 17:14-20). By comparison, the mandate given to man to rule over the earth (Genesis 1:26) is tempered in Genesis 2:15, where man is told to "work" and "take care of" the Garden. The word for "work" here means "to act as a servant."[8]

Putting the argument together, we find that *image*, while it may relate in part to man's nature, has a strong functional component. It means "to act as God's representative on earth, ruling as he rules." This, of course, is tempered by the demand, stressed by Dyrness and many others, that man's rule must never be seen as absolute. It is like that of the kings of Israel who ruled as God's representatives.

If God made the world and declared it to be good, then any action by which man exploits the earth's resources solely for his own ends is prohibited, because it does not represent God. Dyrness writes:

If my thesis—that human dominion is best seen in the ideal rule of Israel's king—is valid, then we should expect that the righteous rule of the king would issue in a productive and fruitful environment, both human and nonhuman.[9]

But we must move deeper. I have argued that creation, in its very essence, was intended to bear two forms of witness: to the glory of the God who made it, and to God's ongoing nurturing care of what he has made.

If Genesis 2:15—"The LORD God took the man and put him in the Garden of Eden to work it and take care of it"—may serve as a model statement of what it means to bear God's image on earth by representing him, we see that *it is our mandate as human beings to enhance creation's witness to the glory and nurture of God.*

As Adam worked the soil, bringing the plant life to the peak of its fertile splendor, he was demonstrating his servanthood at its best. He was declaring before all creation that he accepted the mandate of labor to help nature to testify at full volume concerning the God who formed it. To tend to the Garden was to make it ever more able to point to God as the goal of its praise.

Where was man to fit into the ecological landscape? He was to fit, not as exploiter, but as enhancer of creation's testimony that God is the all-glorious and the ever-nurturing Maker of all that exists.

Here is where our understanding of the biblical response to our current ecological crisis must begin. We were not made to damage the creation, but to enhance its testimony to God. Our activity in the environment was never intended to be sovereign in the sense that we are deities to ourselves, able to do what we want. We were formed in God's image to represent him on earth so that all the earth, in turn, could glorify him better and better.

Every action which has an impact on the environment must be carried out only when we have answered the question: "Will this act enhance or damage creation's ability to glorify God and to testify to his power to nurture what he has made?"

Notes

1. Robert K. Johnston, "Wisdom Literature and its Contribution to a Biblical Environmental Ethic," *Tending the Garden: Essays on the Gospel and the Earth*, ed. Wesley Granberg-Michaelson (Grand Rapids: Wm. B. Eerdmans Publishing Co., 1987), 71. Compare Hans-Jurgen Hermisson, "Observations on the Creation Theology in Wisdom," *Creation in the Old Testament*, ed. Bernhard W. Anderson (Philadelphia: Fortress Press, 1984), 118-34.

2. J. A. Loader, "Image and Order: Old Testament Perspectives on the Ecological Crisis," *Are We Killing God's Earth?: Ecology and Theology*, ed. W. S. Vorster (Pretoria: University of South Africa, 1987), 22.

3. Robert P. Meye, "Invitation to Wonder: Toward a Theology of Nature," *Tending the Garden*, 31.

4. Julian Huxley, *Evolution in Action* (New York: Harper & Row, 1966), 41.

5. Konrad Lorenz, *On Aggression* (London: Methuen, 1966), 201-2; italics are Lorenz's.

6. Edmond Jacob, *Theology of the Old Testament* (London: Hodder & Stoughton, 1958), 167-68. Compare James D. Smart, *The Interpretation of Scripture* (London: SCM Press, 1961), 134-59; Douglas John Hall, *Imaging God* (Grand Rapids: Wm. B. Eerdmans Publishing Co., 1986), 89-113; and Anthony A. Hoekema, *Created in God's Image* (Grand Rapids: Wm. B. Eerdmans Publishing Co., 1986), 78-80.

7. Ibid., 169.

8. William Dyrness, "Stewardship of the Earth in the Old Testament," *Tending the Garden*, 53-54.

9. Ibid., 54.

3

Creation as Victim:
The Dark Witnesses

The first time I really looked at the countryside around Aldergrove, British Columbia, it was an early Sunday morning, and I was on my way to preach a sermon at Aldergrove Baptist Church. The gentle but intensely green farmland, dotted with trees, shimmered in the early morning sun. With the dew glistening in the grass, the mountains as a backdrop, and farm animals here and there awaking to the day, it seemed like a domesticated Eden, a place God would unhesitatingly call "good."

Several years later, I moved to Aldergrove. The scenery was as stunning as ever, but I quickly learned about its darker side. You see, the morning I had first looked at it, the sun had been shining and all nature was displayed at its very best. There was no way then that I could have imagined the same countryside after days of socked-in clouds and endless rain.

When I first saw the dark side, I could not believe that

those brilliant shades of green could turn so somber, that the trees could look so black, that the air could be laden with such a clammy chill. The farmland became hostile, as if it had turned its former bright front away from me to show me its back.

There was no rain in Eden, and the sun probably shone most of the time. But sometime between then and now, the darkness came and nature developed claws. Now, as we look at it with twentieth century eyes, its beauty is mingled with travail and, at times, ferocity. We live in a broken world which we in our wisdom, or lack of it, are quickly making uninhabitable.

When did it happen? When did the forces of darkness invade us? Any reputable Sunday school scholar could answer: It happened when Adam and Eve sinned in the garden. At that moment evil pierced the good and invaded it. When Eve bit into the forbidden fruit, when Adam joined her, could they have foreseen the dreadful complexity they were bringing to the world God made? Before their sin, life was simplicity itself—God had shaped human beings in his image to represent him in a creation which was unadulterated good. All that human beings needed to do was to bring glory to the One who had formed them.

When evil came in, the picture changed, for now creation gave mixed signals. At times the world seemed untouched. At other times it was obvious that a horrible transformation had occurred, so that the environment could scarcely be considered anything but hostile.

Ancient man learned to fear his world. He invented fertility gods and deities of the wind and storm so that, by rituals of appeasement, he could have hope that there would be some regularity to his life. Yet, despite all efforts, he learned by bitter experience that nature was not to be trusted.

Once again we must go back to the beginning in order to understand the dark side of creation and its implications for our present ecological crisis.

Just a Piece of Fruit?

The gentle perfection of Genesis 1 and 2 needs to be seen, ultimately, as a backdrop or stage setting for the tragedy to come. God had arranged everything needed for paradise to be paradise, but humanity unaccountably wanted more. Thus the challenge, "You will be like gods," became the source of all pain, all distress, all sorrow.

Genesis 3 is usually viewed as a spiritual rather than a material phenomenon. The damage Adam and Eve brought upon themselves and passed on to us is most often seen as internal and invisible. But we must recognize that such an interpretation, while partly true, is superficial. Sin has brought corruption to all of life, material and immaterial. The very characteristics of the physical world have been altered radically by the Fall.

Thus it was that Adam, standing bowed before an angry God, heard the chilling words:

"Cursed is the ground because of you;
>through painful toil you will eat of it
>all the days of your life.
It will produce thorns and thistles for you,
>and you will eat the plants of the field.
By the sweat of your brow
>you will eat your food
until you return to the ground,
>since from it you were taken;
for dust you are
>and to dust you will return."

There is an interesting play on words here in that God's

name for the man related to man's origin in the soil. The word *ground* in Hebrew is *Adama*, an echo of *Adam* (man). The curse on the Adam is a curse on the *Adama*, the ground, which is the source of his substance.

What did the fall of Adam and Eve mean for the original plan of God? At its most basic level, it meant that God's determination to nurture what he had formed was qualified, *though not destroyed*. Now the earth would produce only through labor to which Adam was not accustomed. Easy nurture of human crops was a thing of the past.

As well, the earth's testimony to God's glory was qualified, though again not destroyed. The earth brought forth thorns and thistles—enemies, aliens—which would plague humanity for the rest of its earthly existence.

What did the curse mean for the environment? In essence, it meant that the earth became a victim of our sinfulness. James Houston has suggested an analogy which may clarify the new reality of post-Fall existence: "The basic dilemma with nature is that it is only a mirror that casts a reflection of what is projected upon it."[1]

This metaphor tells us two things: First, nature retains its essential goodness and is not to blame for the curse placed upon it. Second, the earth is telling us something, as surely as a quick look in the mirror in the morning tells us if our hair is out of place.

Creation as Mirror

In Romans 8:19-21, Paul offers this comment on the curse of Genesis 3:17-19:

> The creation waits in eager expectation for the sons of God to be revealed. For the creation was subjected to frustration, *not by its own choice*, but by the will of the one who subjected it, in hope

that the creation itself will be liberated from its
bondage to decay and brought into the glorious
freedom of the children of God.[2]

Additional passages affirm in their own way the same
truth—our sin attacks the physical earth, turning it into a
victim against its will (Leviticus 18:25, 28; Isaiah 24:5;
Hosea 4:1-3). There is no sense in which nature is ever to
be viewed as sinful in itself. Instead, it is a mirror of our sin.

The famous story by Oscar Wilde, *The Picture of Dorian
Gray*, provides an admirable illustration. Young Dorian
lived his life to excess. Debauchery was second nature to
him, and every form of fleshly pleasure was his daily diet.
Yet, curiously, he never aged, nor did the side-effects of his
dissipation appear on his features. He was ever youthful.
But secreted away in an attic was a painted portrait of
Dorian Gray, and it was this portrait which aged. Year by
year, *the picture* showed the real Dorian as he would have
been—wrinkled, inflamed, decrepit, moving toward the
grave.

In our world, humanity in its sin appears to move from
one triumph to another. We bear scars, but we hide them
with our optimistic faith in the power of the human mind.
The Bible says we are doomed without Christ, yet few signs
of this show in our daily victories, in our regular advance
toward Utopia. What we have failed to understand is that
we will not find clear indications of coming judgment in
ourselves, for we have masked the evidence. We must, in
our time, look for judgment in the earth, dying before our
eyes. While human beings champion their technology, the
environment reflects the result of their greed and ignorance. The earth is "The Picture of Dorian Gray," made by
God to be perfect, but now on its way to final doom while
mankind remains ever youthful.

Hosea 4:1-3, though speaking to ancient Israel, provides a chilling commentary on our current dilemma:

> Hear the word of the LORD, you Israelites,
>   because the LORD has a charge to bring
>   against you who live in the land:
> "There is no faithfulness, no love,
>   no acknowledgement of God in the land.
> There is only cursing, lying and murder,
>   stealing and adultery;
> they break all bounds,
>   and bloodshed follows bloodshed.
> Because of this the land mourns,
>   and all who live in it waste away;
> the beasts of the field and the birds of the air
>   and the fish of the sea are dying."

Could it be said better? The earth is a mirror. It is the victim of our transgressions.

Sin has defiled the land. Just as the death of certain creatures in the sea is the first warning of a coming ecological disaster, so the entire plight of the earth is a warning—a witness—to a coming catastrophe for all who remain in their sin. What we see in the earth is a mirror of ourselves as God sees us. The earth is our warning that God will not long delay in bringing retribution for our willing rebellion against him.

The Mysterious Ways of God

Sin brings disaster upon the earth. We have seen that. But how does the mechanism work?

In one way, it works directly and obviously. If I dump four quarts of used oil into the ground because I am too lazy to find a proper waste disposal depot, I have polluted it, and my neighbors may reap the benefits. If a society fouls its environment because of ignorance or greed, its sin turns creation into a victim.

But the mechanism is far more complex than that. Here we encounter the God who, no matter how well we come to know him, embodies mysteries which seem unaccountable. God made this earth and declared it good in his eyes. In turn, the earth sang to him. It gave him glory and proclaimed his gracious power to nurture all that he had made.

When sin entered, however, a change occurred, a transformation in the Creator's dealings with nature. Most of us would label it incredible, for *God became a defiler of the earth.* He turned around and attacked the creation he had so lovingly formed, diminishing its witnesses both to his glory and to his power to nurture. He became an ecological enemy.

Before we dismiss this analysis as the ranting of a biblical scholar run amuck, let's consider the evidence.

The Curse. In Genesis 3:17, God said, "Cursed is the ground because of you." Who cursed the ground? God did. And as the rest of the passage goes on to affirm, he did so because he intended to limit the earth's power to nurture Adam (compare Genesis 5:29). Romans 8:19-21, quoted earlier, reaffirms our conclusion: Creation was subjected to frustration *by God.*

The Flood. In the face of multiplied sins of rebellious mankind, God brought about a cataclysm that eliminated most of the world's life. It must have taken centuries for the earth to recover fully from the things God did to it in that time. Peter says that the sinners of his day "deliberately forget that long ago by God's word the heavens existed and the earth was formed out of water and by water. By these waters also the world of that time was deluged and destroyed" (2 Peter 3:5-6). The implication is obvious: the same God who made the world exercised his right to destroy it by means of the very substance out of which it had been formed.[3]

The Covenant Curse. A further evidence of God's attack on nature comes from the "covenant curse" of the Old Testament. The Lord made a covenant with his people, an agreement which stipulated that, in return for their obedience, they would have God's perpetual grace, protection, and blessing. The covenant, however, had real teeth to it. In Deuteronomy 28:15-68, the Creator decreed horrific judgments if his people broke the terms of the covenant which they had pledged with a blood-oath to obey.

Of special interest to us is the degree to which the covenant curse was to involve nature. The curse included drought (vv. 22-24), mildew on crops (v. 22), devouring locusts and worms (vv. 38-42), and enemy armies which would wipe out crops and livestock (vv. 49-51). In other words, under God's judgment the role of the land as a supportive environment would be virtually eliminated, and the people would be left without the resources vital for survival.

This, in fact, did occur. In direct response to the apostasy of his people, God brought severe droughts and mildew (1 Kings 16:29-17:1; Haggai 1:10-11; 2:17). He made their lives as precarious as life could be. And, as often as not, the instruments of his judgment were invading armies, who pursued a scorched earth policy in order to render the people of God helpless. The Book of Joel provides a valuable summary of the effect on nature of God's condemnation of his people. Whether the reference of the prophecy is to a literal locust attack or to human enemy attack, the result is the same: stripped trees and vines (1:7, 12), ruined fields (1:10), farm animals without pasture (1:18), and wild beasts without water (1:20).[4]

The evidence is obvious and clear. God, who made a perfect world to glorify him and proclaim his nurturing care, has, since the Fall, attacked the world he made, diminishing its witness both to glory and to nurture. Why? What possible benefit could come from the Creator turning, seemingly, into an ecological enemy?

THE DARK WITNESSES

Such questions do have answers, though they are not as straightforward as we might hope. Sin has brought complexity into our world, and God has responded in a complex way. Perhaps the best approach to an understanding of God's mysterious attack on creation is to look at it again as a witness. Now, however, the witnesses we will be considering are dark and negative, despite their significant purposes.

To the two initial bright testimonies borne by the world God made—glory and nurture—he has added, since the Fall, two dark witnesses—penalty and precariousness.

Third Witness: Penalty

Romans 6:23 affirms that the wages of sin is death. In the time of the Fall of man, this quickly proved to be true: Adam and Eve's embarrassment over their nakedness led to the slaughter of animals to provide them with clothing (Genesis 3:21).

Up to the point of the first human sin, there was an eternal youth in the created order, a sense that nothing God made would grow old or fail. But the Fall eventually brought physical death upon Adam, Eve, and their first offspring. It also inaugurated a new cycle of life and death in all of the created world.

Beyond this, there were many small deaths to be faced—crops that failed, illnesses that brought men low, and countless other trials and tribulations to cast down the faint of heart. The comment of Jacob upon his own life could well be a litany for much of humanity: "My years have been few and difficult" (Genesis 47:9).

If creation truly is a mirror, we must look for the meaning of the harshness of life in ourselves. And it is there. God has stated a clear relationship between sin and death, whether physical or spiritual (Romans 5:12; 1 Corinthians 15:56). What we see in creation in the form of the curse on the ground, and ultimately on all life forms, is but an echo of the spiritual curse resting on our inner beings.

God, in his wisdom, has determined that we will have a visible demonstration of our greatest problem—that we are rebels, estranged from God, and doomed to eternal judgment unless we surrender to him. If we cannot see in our own hearts that the wages of sin is death (not to mention the pain on the way to death), we will see it every day in the creation around us.

Our world is dangerous. No one should be able to look at it without discovering the truth about it, that, just as the creation is often warped and harsh, so we human beings have gone wrong and there is a penalty to be paid. God will not ignore sin but will judge us with all the tribulation it takes to bring us to our senses and to force us to acknowledge the truth about ourselves.

Whether it is the Old Testament covenant curse, or the curse we have brought on our own heads by polluting our world, there is always a price to be paid for sin and a repentance required. In this regard, Romans 1:32 has importance, though it has puzzled theologians. Referring to people without a specific written revelation from God, it declares: "Although they know God's righteous decree that those who do such things deserve death, they not only continue to do these very things but also approve of those who practice them." Earlier in Romans 1, Paul affirmed that people even without the Scriptures know God because they see the creation he made (1:18-20). But how do such people gain the knowledge that sin is to be punished with death?

Obviously, all people have a conscience which, to a greater or lesser degree, gives an understanding of right and wrong. But this is not enough to show that sin leads to death. Rather, it is the third witness of creation itself—the dark witness of penalty—which provides mankind with the knowledge that doom comes to those who oppose God by their deeds.

As human beings look at the world under the curse, as they are from time to time betrayed by a creation with claws, they see their own reflection. Though they may deny what they are seeing, the testimony remains always before them and they are without excuse (Romans 1:20).

Fourth Witness: Precariousness

The fallen world does not simply convey an intellectual knowledge that sin brings penalty. It also transmits to mankind a testimony which strikes deeper, into the hidden fears of all of us.

In the Garden, Adam and Eve existed within the assurance that they could go on living forever, eternally nurtured by the protecting and sustaining God. Only when they were thrown out of the Garden did nature become hostile, with death awaiting at the end of the road. The contrast could not have been greater. One day they were secure. The next day they were thrust into the terrifying realm of precariousness, where nothing seemed certain or permanent any longer.

Why does God bring such insecurity into the creation he formed? Why does he allow creation to frighten us as it so often does? It is not because his vindictiveness is out of control but because he has a higher goal—our redemption. To grasp the meaning of the dark witness of precariousness, consider the concrete example of the all too common phenomenon of the natural disaster, the so-called "act of God."

In the face of earthquakes, floods, hurricanes, and other seemingly freakish and capricious happenings in our world, the popular theologians have had a field day. "Is it God's fault?" they ask, "or Satan's?" Is the community buried under a landslide more sinful than the community that finds a large gold deposit within city limits?

Jesus had something to say about those moments of tragedy when nature lashes out seemingly at random. He referred to a tower which collapsed, killing eighteen people (Luke 13:4). Whether it fell because of an earthquake or a strong wind or the natural processes of decay is irrelevant. The crucial thing is that eighteen bystanders, minding their own business, were crushed to death in an instant.

Jesus' question went to the heart of the issue: Were these eighteen more wicked than anyone else in Jerusalem? His answer was, "No." The real lesson of the fallen tower was not that natural disasters help us to find the worst sinners, but that the fallen world offers no guarantees. Any of us can be snuffed out at any moment by a wide variety of means. Thus we must all repent so that we are ready at any moment to die.

There is an apparent difference between the man who shakes his fist at God and is immediately struck by lightning and someone who walks past a tower and is buried under twenty tons of rock. In the first instance, we have a witness of *penalty*—creation used by God to judge the specific sin of a specific sinner. When a tower falls on you, however, or an earthquake buries you, or a flash flood sweeps you away, the testimony seems of a different order—the witness of *precariousness*, communicating that life after the fall is insecure, without a solid foundation.

Yet, the two witnesses work in tandem, so that our distinguishing of them may be purely academic. Sin brings penalty which brings precariousness. Whether or not we can point to a specific penalty brought against us for a specific sin may not be relevant. The crucial point is that creation is speaking to us, saying that we are in mortal danger unless we are made right with God.

Perhaps the greatest statement of the physical world regarding penalty and precariousness is the phenomenon of death. Death is at the heart of the anxiety of our age. The reason is obvious—death is the ultimate natural disaster. It attacks all living things, often without sufficient warning, regardless of the depth of depravity or the height of righteousness in a certain age. Whether it is a house plant that dies before its time, or a crop beaten to pulp by a hailstorm, or the decay and collapse of our own bodies, creation now bears witness to far more than the glory of God. It announces that sin demands a price to be paid and that human transgression attacks our security in the world God made.

The question is not: "Why does God use creation to attack us in this way?" The real question is: "What is the *intention* of the dark witnesses?"

The answer to the latter question is not at all complex. God simply wants to drive us back into his arms. He knows that the bane of our existence is our foolish self-sufficiency which leads us to exclaim, "Who needs God?" He does not want us to be self-secure, for we were not made to exist successfully except under his lordship.

Ultimately, even as the witness of penalty is intended to reveal to us our true condition as doomed people needing redemption, so the goal of the tandem witness of precariousness is to drive us back to God who, above all things in this world, is the only One who is secure.

As Jesus put it in commenting on the fallen tower: "Unless you repent, you too will all perish." The precariousness of the physical creation is only a mirror of the precariousness of our very existence before an angry God. Perhaps if we are frightened enough, some of us will run back to our Rock, our only Refuge, and be saved.

FOUR WITNESSES: A CONTRADICTION?

We have now viewed both the bright and the dark sides of nature. In its simplicity before that Fall, creation bore two bright testimonies—to the glory of the majestic God who had made it and to the nurturing power of the Creator. With mankind's sin two more witnesses, dark and forbidding, intruded—penalty and precariousness.

But is this not essentially a contradiction? If we wanted to, we could view *penalty* as the direct opposite of *glory*, for the former involves God striking the earth so that it reveals ugliness. When penalty is at work, God's glory is veiled, except as it relates to his sovereign might to judge sinners. In the same way, *precariousness* and *nurture* can be seen as opposites. Where there is nurture, there is security; where there is precariousness, there is insecurity.

Can God really be saying opposing things through the same creation and still use creation to bear an effective witness? Is he not simply confusing us?

The answer lies in understanding how the witnesses came to be. The bright witnesses—glory and nurture—were there from the first. In a way, they had nothing to do with us. Even if there was no humanity, the earth would still proclaim God's glory and nurturing power.

But the dark witnesses are God's response to human sin. They are, if you will, painted onto the canvas which originally demonstrated only the bright witnesses. The bright witnesses are diminished, to be sure, but they remain the original testimonies of creation. The dark witnesses, by contrast, are intruders.

As mankind looks at all four witnesses, there is an intuitive understanding of how they work. People instinctively grasp the truth that glory and nurture are primary, closer to the One who made the earth. This is why we so readily flock to the great outdoors, expecting it to renew our spirits.

We all somehow grasp as well the second truth that penalty and precariousness are intruders, that they do not belong here. It is a sad reality that most of those who reject God's ways choose to block out what they understand about the dark witnesses—that they are intended to wake us up and drive us back to God. But if even some begin to understand their need for God, the dark testimonies are worth the pain they bring.

Ultimately the four witnesses are not a contradiction, because they all have the same purpose. If we will not praise the Maker because we see in creation his glory and nurture, then perhaps we will run to him in terror when we understand the curse on our lives and the precariousness of our existence.

God has a plan. All of the witnesses are, in the final analysis, his grace-gifts, for they are the Creator's call: "Return to me."

THE DARK WITNESSES
AND THE ECOLOGICAL CRISIS

Despite the seemingly good purpose of the dark witnesses, we cannot get away from the fact that God deliberately damages the world he made, that he attacks it with fore-thought. If God is to be seen as an ecological enemy, what hope can there be for us to emulate a higher purpose—to preserve the world God created?

Some in evangelical circles have justified the exploita-tion of our world by reasoning that the earth is cursed any-way. Why should we protect it if God does not? This problem is not to be dismissed lightly. We will return to it several times before our study is done.

As a clue to a solution, perhaps we should begin to con-sider the mandate given to humanity—"Work the gar-den"—in contrast to God's self-imposed mandate to do what is required to bring us back to him. In using the curse as an excuse to damage the earth, have we taken up the mandate which belongs solely to Another?

A second clue to a response to God's dark work in this world comes from a recognition that even here, in his dealings with creation, he acts with a complexity that makes simple solutions impossible. For even as he attacks what he has made, he continues to tend it like a garden.

Notes

1. James M. Houston, *I Believe in the Creator* (Grand Rapids: Wm. B. Eerdmans Publishing Co., 1980), 30-31.

2. Throughout the history of the church there have been those who have argued that this passage does not refer to nonhuman creation but to lost human beings. See F. Godet, *Commentary on the Epistle to the Romans* (Grand Rapids: Zondervan Publishing House, 1956; reprint of 1883 ed.), 313-14. Godet rejected this view for the following reasons: "For of two things one or the other must happen: either they will be

converted before the expected time, and in that case they will themselves be found among the children of God, and will not form part of the *creation* (end of the verse and verse 21). Or if they are not converted, they will not participate in the glorious condition of the children of God" (313).

3. The long-held argument that God lifted the curse on the ground after the flood is based on an interpretive error (see the most recent proponent of this view: Wesley Granberg-Michaelson, "Earthkeeping: A Theology for Global Sanctification," *Sojourners*, October 1982, 21-24). While Genesis 8:21 does reveal God's promise never again to curse the ground because of man, this statement is in parallel with another promise never again to destroy life with a flood. Thus the curse referred to in this verse is specific: a curse by flooding the earth. There is no lifting of the general curse against the earth. This conclusion is supported by most commentators.

4. The plagues against Egypt (Exodus 7:14-11:10) show a similar pattern of judgment by God on the enemies of his people.

4

Creation under Grace

I will sing for the one I love
    a song about his vineyard:
My loved one had a vineyard
    on a fertile hillside.
He dug it up and cleared it of stones
    and planted it with the choicest vines.
He built a watchtower in it
    and cut out a winepress as well.
Then he looked for a crop of good grapes,
    but it yielded only bad fruit.

"Now you dwellers in Jerusalem
    and men of Judah,
    judge between me and my vineyard.
What more could I have done for my vineyard
    than I have done for it?
When I looked for good grapes,
    why did it yield only bad?" (Isaiah 5:1-4)

This nature parable, a foreshadowing of the teachings of Jesus, refers to God's people: The vineyard is Israel (Isaiah 5:7) and the keeper of the vineyard is the Creator. Though we cannot see Isaiah 5 as a model for the Creator's wise care of agricultural land, it does present the possibility of a striking parallel between human action and the environment.

In the first part of the parable, we have a metaphor which describes God as working in the midst of his people to bring out the best in them. If the account were to be taken literally, the parable would show the way in which the Maker enables his physical world to proclaim his glory and to produce in abundance. But it seems so obvious that this is a metaphorical description of Israel that we naturally view it as a parable without any real reference to the physical creation.

The passage has a dark side. When all efforts on the part of the vineyard keeper fail, and the fruit of the vineyard (Israel) is only continually bad, God announces:

> "Now I will tell you
>   what I am going to do to my vineyard:
> I will take away its hedge,
>   and it will be destroyed;
> I will break down its wall,
>   and it will be trampled.
> I will make it a wasteland,
>   neither pruned nor cultivated,
>   and briers and thorns will grow there.
> I will command the clouds
>   not to rain on it." (Isaiah 5:5-6)

Again the language is that of metaphor. Isaiah 5:7 shows clearly that the vineyard is Israel. Yet two important facts compel us to look at the passage more closely. First, the description of the judgment on the vineyard closely parallels the covenant curse God had reserved for the physical land of the Israelites when they sinned (Deuteronomy 28:15-24). If God's people were to fall under condemnation, the means God would use would be to make their territory a "wasteland" and to "command the clouds not to rain on it."

Second, Isaiah 5 does not simply contain a parable. The chapter moves on to respond to a situation in which the Israelites, motivated by greed, were consolidating large land holdings at the expense of their fellow citizens. In answering this sin, God declared:

> "Surely the great houses will become desolate,
>   the fine mansions left without occupants.
> A ten-acre vineyard will produce only
>   a bath of wine,
>   a homer of seed only an ephah of grain."
>
> (Isaiah 5:9b-10)

This is not a metaphor. Now we find God judging sin by striking the actual land of his people. Is it a coincidence that he attacks their vineyards, or is he linking his earlier parable to a real physical judgment on the fruit of the vine?

We have seen that what is done in the world of humankind is mirrored in the creation. If we will not obey God because we see his glory and nurturing power in the created order, we may turn to him when his attack on what he has made testifies to penalty and precariousness.

This is exactly what the Maker is teaching in both the parable of the vineyard (Isaiah 5:1-6) and his pronouncement against Israel's actual vineyards (Isaiah 5:10). God has brought abundant life to his creation to demonstrate his majesty and his ability to provide for creation's needs.

When mankind rejects his obvious statement to them, he brings their physical environment crashing down as a dark witness against them.

Because we see this phenomenon in the concrete part of the chapter (5:10), we are justified in seeing Isaiah 5:1-6 as more than a parable about people. It is in its own way a statement about God's relationship with creation itself, the physical world mirroring the spiritual condition of his people.

What may we understand from it? First, we need to see that Isaiah 5 is describing creation after the Fall, for it has the potential of yielding either good or bad crops. Second, this is God's vineyard, and he does everything needed to make it produce abundantly. There is loving care involved here despite the obvious fallenness of the land he is working. Third, *only when the bright witnesses have been continually rejected are the dark witnesses brought into play.*

In the last chapter, we posed the question: Why should we care for creation if even God attacks it? The answer we suggested was that *care* for the creation is our mandate. We have no mandate to damage what God made. Only the Maker has the right to do that.

Now we must move to a more powerful reason: *The destruction of the vineyard is not God's primary intention.* God has not simply moved from using bright witnesses before the Fall to advancing dark witnesses after the Fall. His first work is still to demonstrate his glory and to nurture his world, even though the Fall has occurred.

Learning from Luther

Martin Luther, throughout his writings and sermons, made a careful distinction between two activities of God—his "proper" work and his "strange" (or "alien") work. The former relates to the Creator's plan to bless the people he made, to nurture them in every way. The latter, the "strange" work, involves judgment and chastisement for sin.

Luther's unusual terminology for God's strange work came directly from Scripture. In speaking of God's judgment on Israel (here called "Ephraim"), Isaiah writes:

> The LORD will rise up as he did at
>   Mount Perazim,
>   he will rouse himself as in the
>   Valley of Gibeon—
> to do his work, his strange work,
>   and perform his task, his alien task.
>   (Isaiah 28:21)

Why is it strange? Why alien? According to Luther, all Scripture makes the answer plain. God's proper work is to save, to redeem, to bless. This has been his constant plan since creation. His strange work, on the other hand is condemnation. We must not, however, see the judgment of God as merely vindictive, as if he were saying, "Let me bless you as you obey me, or I will destroy you." Instead, he appeals to us, "Let me save you with my love and grace, or I will seek to save you with my harshness." In both cases, the goal is salvation. Only those who utterly reject all of his work for their salvation will be finally and eternally condemned.

Let us allow Luther to speak to this important doctrine:

> Although he is the God of life and salvation and
> this is his proper work, yet, in order to accom-
> plish this, he kills and destroys. These works are
> alien to him, but through them he accomplishes
> his proper work. For he kills our will that his
> may be established in us. He subdues the flesh
> and its lusts that the spirit and its desires may
> come to life.[1]

God calls out to us: "What more could have been done for my vineyard than I have done for it?" (Isaiah 5:4). Only when he has done all that grace—the bright witnesses—could do to communicate to us, does he bring in the dark witnesses. Even as creation mirrors our sin, it far more greatly and more constantly mirrors God's glory and his desire to nurture what he has made.

The simple view that the physical creation before the Fall was under blessing and after the Fall is under judgment, will not do. The Creator only pulls out judgment, the dark witnesses, when we go on refusing to be convicted by his blessing. It is only when we look at all that God has made and continue to insist that he did not make it or that we owe him nothing that the creation turns on us with ferocity.

If this analysis is correct, we should see, even in Scripture, that the bright witnesses are dominant in God's plan to win us back to him. As long as there is hope of redemption, God's glory and nurturing power should continue to be found as the strongest testimonies of the created order.

Limits on the Fall of Creation

Despite the Fall, God has not written off the world he made. The Greek notion that physical matter is evil misses the point. Creation has always remained good, even when used as the mirror of human sin. Even in the midst of the curse, creation has never been allowed to abandon its original purpose, never been permitted to turn out the lights on its bright witnesses.

Scripture rejoices in creation, in its beauty and glory, Fall or no Fall. So, far from writing it off, God himself continues to rejoice in and to protect the world he created.

Consider his covenant after the dark witnesses had performed the terrible work of the Flood. God did not relate the promises of his covenant just to mankind. The contract was also made with "every living creature on earth" (Genesis 9:10). Central to it was a pledge never again to wipe out living things through a flood, as if God were saying, "Once is enough to make the point. Now I will protect my creation from being used in that way again."

Psalm 104 presents a marvelous picture of God reveling in the world he formed. Whether he is providing water for all living things (vv. 10-13), or produce from the earth (v. 14), or wine, oil, and bread for man (v. 15), or trees for the birds (vv. 16-17), or mountain crags for goats and badgers (v. 18), or prey for the carnivorous beasts (vv. 20-21), God orchestrates the functioning of his world with a music which no symphony could ever hope to imitate. Walter Harrelson writes on Psalm 104: "The bounty of God; the outpouring of his goodness and plenty, go beyond what is essential to maintain life."[2]

This is a work of love, of grace despite what needs to be done when the dark witnesses are called for. Taken in its totality, God's work is not, ultimately, that of an ecological enemy. If he hurts his world to communicate essential truth to us, he works doubly or triply well to enhance the bright witnesses. He loves his creation and thus carefully limits the effects of the Fall.

A Plan for Restoration

We are well aware that the curse upon humanity, brought about because of sin, was not intended to be irrevocable. God immediately set about to establish a plan for man's salvation. He instituted a holy line through Seth (Genesis 4:25-26), culminating in the Creator's call to Abraham to be the founding father of the chosen people (Genesis 12:1-3).

It is a general consensus today that the statement in

Genesis 12:3—"and all the peoples on earth will be blessed through you"—demonstrates that God intended to use his relationship with Israel to entice humanity in general to himself. The chosen people were not to be some self-congratulating holy huddle, but a missionary people, proclaiming the glory and nurturing power of God so that the nations would turn their hearts back to the Creator.

The bright witnesses of creation were to be dominant over the dark witnesses. God intends his world to testify more powerfully to glory and nurture than to penalty and precariousness. Since God, after the Fall, began to work for the restoration of humanity, and since creation is humanity's mirror, dare we hope that God also intended in some way to restore the physical creation?

Scripture makes it evident that this was exactly the Maker's intention, especially as we find it in his work with the chosen people after their escape from Egypt. God had promised the children of Israel centuries before their captivity ended that he would return his people to their own land. The first spies who reported back to the Israelites in the time of the Exodus announced that the land God had deeded to them was flowing with milk and honey.

It was no wonderful coincidence that the Promised Land of God's people was known for its fertility. The Creator had made it so. As the followers of Moses and then Joshua moved from desert to abundance, their experience became a definite expression of the reality that the earth is a mirror of the people who inhabit it.

Earlier, in the desert, the Israelites had accepted the covenant of God, pledging to be obedient to him in all things (Exodus 24:7-8). If the people's pledge could have been lived out perfectly, they would have had an existence similar to that of Adam and Eve before the Fall. Even when Israel demonstrated her obvious imperfections, God revealed a continuing intention to make her environment in the Promised Land testify through bright witnesses rather than dark ones.

In particular, the witness of nurture came to the fore. As Israel obeyed God, she received from him the promise of fertile security:

> The LORD will grant you abundant prosperity—in the fruit of your womb, the young of your livestock and the crops of your ground—in the land he swore to your forefathers to give you.
>
> The LORD will open the heavens, the storehouse of his bounty, to send rain on your land in season and to bless all the work of your hands. (Deuteronomy 28:11-12a)

Notice the promise of fertility, something the Fall had denied to mankind. Israel was to be a sign of redemption, of restoration, in essence of a return to the Garden. Her fertility was to act as a visible mirror of the invisible truth that God and his people had come to terms and that the rebellion of humanity was beginning to unravel.

William Dumbrell has written:

> In Deuteronomy the promised land is extravagantly idealized. It is the very quintessence of fertility and fruitfulness. There is nothing lacking in it. . . . One can hardly escape the impression that what is being depicted through such references is Eden recaptured, paradise recovered.[3]

Dumbrell cites as evidence Deuteronomy 7:14-15; 8:7; and 11:11-12.

In the land promised to Israel forever, the bright witnesses were to glow as beacons pointing to the God who not only creates, who not only condemns, but who also restores. This, of course, was based on an ideal in which the spiritual promises of his people were kept and treasured, in which Israel's praises to God's glory and nurture were constantly on her lips.

Even a quick study of Deuteronomy 28, the famous "blessing and cursing" chapter, shows that the bounty of the land was available only if God's people kept the covenant he had issued to them. Disobedience would bring the covenant curse, embodied in the dark witnesses, into play.

God's Ecology Program

If we are not to see God as predominantly an ecological enemy (though the environment may be used by him as a weapon of judgment), can we view him as a wise ecologist primarily concerned to enhance what he has made? Was his plan to restore Eden in the land of his faithful people a genuine proposal or had he already written off his fallen world? Are the bright witnesses truly intended to shine through the dark ones?

As far as Scripture is concerned, God's first and most dominant desire was genuine restoration. Several lines of evidence point to the same conclusion. First, the Creator firmly declared that the earth was his (Psalm 24:1). He included in his claim the land of his own people, for they were to consider themselves to be tenants (Leviticus 25:23). This meant that free exploitation of the creation by sinful human beings was not to go unpunished, for the land was held in trust, not owned outright. Here, of course, we see a renewal of the original mandate to "work the Garden," to preserve it and enhance its bright witnesses (Genesis 2:15). Since creation is God's, we dare not abuse it but must affirm it.

Second, God himself continued to care for creation, to nurture it. Psalm 145:13-16 declares the Maker's faithfulness to and ongoing love for all he has made. We have already remarked on Psalm 104, where all life receives its sustenance from God. The Maker, far from abandoning his fallen world, remained its caring provider.

Third, God set down laws by which his people were to maintain an ecological sensitivity. Here the goal was to make the land of the Israelites, the potentially restored Eden, as productive as possible. While it is apparent that Israel learned much of her agricultural skill from her neighbors (for example, terracing and the use of dung for fertilizer),[4] it is equally clear that her ecological consciousness was strongly influenced by her Maker's regulations for use of the land.

Foundational to God's agricultural laws was the use of fallowing. According to the Creator's decree, for one full year in seven (the Sabbath Year), Israel was to plant no crops but allow the land to rest and have its nutrients replenished. Once every fifty years (the Jubilee), a further year of rest was ordered, and land previously sold to others was to revert to its original owners (Leviticus 25:1-17).

While Israel, as a matter of good agriculture, appears to have practiced fallowing on a more or less regular basis, year by year,[5] the specific command of the Sabbath Year had several ecological purposes. First, it reminded the Israelites that the land did not belong to them—the orders for its care came from the true owner. As Walter Brueggemann puts it, "Sabbath is for honoring land,"[6] that is, recognizing its true meaning as a trust from God. Second, God ensured that a minimum fallowing process was decreed so that the land would not be burned out by excessive agriculture. Third, the stipulation of the Jubilee (fiftieth) Year of rest, that all land was to revert to its original owner, militated in favor of small landholdings controlled by families rather than super-farms where ecological control was not as carefully monitored.

This latter purpose had some interesting ramifications. Archaeology has discovered that the description of God in his vineyard (Isaiah 5:1-4, quoted at the beginning of this chapter) models the family farm of the time. Such farms were carefully maintained "bread baskets" in which wise agricultural methods produced bountiful harvests. These small landholdings existed by the hundreds, especially around Jerusalem.[7]

When, however, the opportunities came for agricultural export in the time of the kings, there was a tendency to amalgamate land into larger holdings. Family farms sold out to big business. Hopkins has put forward solid evidence to show that export of oil and wine intensified greatly in the eighth century B.C.[8] We have at least one passage—2 Chronicles 26:10—which shows King Uzziah governing vast amalgamated agricultural plots worked by the common people.

The condemnation of Isaiah 5:8 makes sense in this context:

> Woe to you who add house to house
>   and join field to field
> till no space is left
>   and you live alone in the land.

Such activity removed property from family control where ecological concerns had to be upheld or the family would starve, and moved it into the realm of intensive farming where the loss of an acre or ten due to neglect would not be as keenly felt.

As well, the demands of export probably militated against the correct use of fallowing techniques. The fallow system and the Jubilee Year fell apart as God's people moved deeper into sin under the reign of wicked kings. Leviticus 26:32-34 had warned of this danger, and 2 Chronicles 36:21 shows that the warning was justified: "The land enjoyed its Sabbath rests [which, by implication, it had not been enjoying]; all the time of its desolation it rested, until the seventy years were completed in fulfillment of the word of the LORD spoken by Jeremiah."

It is plain from the Scriptures, despite the lack of a great deal of detailed ecological instruction, that God expected his people to live wisely in the land. His overall purpose was to allow the territory of Israel to flourish and even become a remade Eden, and he judged all attempts to thwart that purpose.

Holiness, the Supreme Ecological Imperative

Yet ultimately it was not the methods by which the Israelites maintained the land in fruitfulness that determined the ecological health of the Jewish nation. It was their faithfulness to God's supreme imperative that they live before him as holy people.

Here the fascinating analysis of Walter Brueggemann's *The Land* has much to commend it. Brueggemann uses Deuteronomy 17:16-17's instruction to future kings of Israel to demonstrate the ecological importance of faithfulness to God. Since the land was a gift, held in trust, the kings were not to multiply precious metals and horses, building security for themselves. Rather, their security was to be in God, the giver of the land and the ultimate Guarantor of its fertility. Further, the kings were to be subjected to the law of God instead of living in anxiety about whether or not the land in their care would produce.[9]

It was not that the Israelites were to live in careless

laziness, for the law itself set down rules concerning the working of the soil. Rather, as they labored under ecologically sensitive ground-rules, they had to remind themselves constantly that it was God alone who could guarantee their prosperity. Brueggemann writes:

> The new land, the land given beyond Jordan, the land of restoration, is land by graciousness. And therefore the land shall be secure and life-giving. It is land where security does not need to be manufactured, where well-being need not come by conjuring and calculation. Here security and well-being are not from the grudging task-master, but from the benevolent rain-sender, the same one who was bread-giver. Both rain and manna come from heaven, from outside the history of coercion and demand.[10]

This significant analysis tells us two things of importance for our biblical analysis of ecology. First, as we have affirmed throughout this chapter, God's primary intention, even after the Fall, was to let the bright witnesses shine. His people were to model before the nations a land which trumpeted God's glory and his nurturing care. Second, the power of man to promote the nurturing work of the land in his own strength was to be curtailed severely. The Promised Land's agricultural treasures were not to be won by strife and labor, for then there would be room for boasting and a lurking sense of self-sufficiency. As Deuteronomy 8:10-18 warns, such an attitude would take away from proper glorification of God.

Above all, no hope of a renewed Eden could survive the continued disobedience of the chosen people. All of the promises to Israel concerning God's desire to cause the bright witnesses to triumph over the dark ones were conditional.

And here lies the heart of the tragedy, for Israel chose the path of rebellion and thus moved herself into the realm of broken dreams. She abandoned her Eden for a foolish crusade into the desert of "freedom" from God. And, in so doing, she became the story of all humanity in its sin.

The Land in Crisis

We do not live in Eden, even if we occasionally glimpse it through the rainbow spray of a waterfall or the hues of a sunset.

We live beyond the curse, in a world which has forgotten God. Was there a time when our faithfulness might have brought us the blessings of a new Garden? Perhaps, though our experience labels us unrepentant and thus doomed without Christ.

Of one thing we can be certain: God began with every good intention, even after the Fall, of shoving the dark witnesses behind him and shining forth with his glory and nurture. But we rejected him and now live in a world where the light is fading quickly. Soon it will be night.

Ultimately our problem is not ecological, a matter of the neglect of available technology and of a greed for maximum profit. Our problem is spiritual. The earth merely echoes our condition before a holy and increasingly angry God.

He is not to blame for our plight. Let us understand that clearly. Ever since the Fall, God has sought the restoration of the earth, not its destruction. But his blessing ultimately depends on our response to him. That response, despite all that he has done, remains predominantly negative.

Sadly, and with no sense of self-accusation, God asks:

"What more could I have done for my vineyard than I have done for it?"

Finally, God's patience comes to an end. Then it is time for the dark witnesses to be alive in the earth.

Notes

1. Martin Luther, "Psalm 2," *Luther's Works, Vol. 14: Selected Psalms III* (St. Louis: Concordia Publishing House, 1958), 335. Compare his "Sermon on St. Thomas' Day, Ps. 19:1, December 21, 1516," *Luther's Works, Vol. 51, Sermons* (Philadelphia: Fortress Press, 1959), 18-19.

2. Walter Harrelson, "On God's Care for the Earth: Psalm 104," *Currents in Theology and Mission*, 2, February 1975, 20.

3. William J. Dumbrell, *Covenant and Creation: A Theology of Old Testament Covenants* (Nashville: Thomas Nelson Publishers, 1984), 120.

4. For further information on terracing, by which hillsides were reshaped for agriculture through intricate systems of retaining walls, see Lawrence E. Stager, "The Archaeology of the East Slope of Jerusalem and the Terraces of Kidron," *Journal of Near Eastern Studies*, 41, 1982, 111-12. Gershon Edelstein and Shimon Gibson, "Ancient Jerusalem's Rural Food Basket," *Biblical Archaeology Review*, 8, July/August 1982, 46-54, (has a number of illustrations of terracing methods).

5. See Frank S. Frick, *The Formation of the State in Ancient Israel: A Survey of Models and Theories* (Sheffield, Eng.: Almond Press, 1985), 152; and David C. Hopkins, "The Dynamics of Agriculture in Monarchical Israel," *Society of Biblical Literature 1983 Seminar Papers*, ed. Kent Harold Richards (Chico, Calif.: Scholars Press, 1983), 185-86.

6. Walter Brueggemann, *The Land* (Philadelphia: Fortress Press, 1977), 64.

7. For a description with illustrations, see Edelstein and Gibson, "Ancient Jerusalem's Rural Food Basket," 46-54.

8. Hopkins, "Dynamics of Agriculture," 198-200.

9. Brueggemann, *The Land*, 75-78.

10. Ibid., 50-51.

5

Creation's Destiny

I came upon it suddenly—a grove of death. Slender sagging trees clothed in a dusty shroud of what must have been green needles and brown bark. One moment I had been trudging rather mindlessly through the forest, oblivious to the sounds of squirrels and birds.

Now I was awake, and there were no birds. There was no life at all except for a few bugs of the type that survive nuclear wars. The contrast between what I had left and what I had entered was shocking. I was standing on an acre or two of dead planet.

What had killed this particular spot while the rest of the forest thrived? My experience as a naturalist is minimal so that I will, perhaps, never know. But to me it was a sign that will trouble me all my life. *This world may as easily die as live, given the right conditions.*

We can become rather callous about the loss of a few small patches of the immense globe we live on. Yet we must be sensitive to the testimonies spoken by our world, even those we would rather ignore. The dark witnesses are alive and, if Scripture is predicting accurately, our planet is beginning to unravel. We may well be the very generation that watches it move to the conclusion of the process.

The Specter of Uncreation

The bright witnesses were intended by God to be dominant. Where penalty and precariousness were seen in Scripture, they more often lurked in the wings than took center stage.

Now we must consider a theme which all of us would rather shut away in some dark closet. It is a topic which relates most closely to the way in which God's patience and justice are intertwined.

We have seen that God's proper work is blessing and his strange and less common work is condemnation for sin. God's patience has been the reason for the survival of rebellious humanity, since a Maker more quick to judge would have wiped us all out long ago. But his patience has limits. We cannot continue laughing in the face of God forever. One day justice will be done, and those of us who have stood defiantly in the wrong camp will know that God keeps all of his promises, even the grim ones.

It is here that his ongoing warnings—which we have labeled the "dark witnesses"—are so crucial. Though God has always promoted nature's testimony of glory and nurture as his primary signs to us, most of humanity continues to ignore him and to grow even more sinful. For those who are willing to be honest with the Scriptures, there are clear signs that the dark witnesses have long been preparing for such an eventuality.

Woven through the tragic story of Israel's failure in the

Old Testament, and even through the victorious account of a new beginning in Christ, we find moments when the dark witnesses have swarmed together to bring unprecedented disaster on a particular generation. What do such events communicate? Put quite simply, *they are awesome warnings from God that, given the unrepentance of man, one day he will in judgment uncreate all that he has made.* He will turn it back into the barrenness from which it came, and the dark witnesses, at least for that moment, will triumph.

As we look at Scripture's stern warning of uncreation at the hands of the united dark witnesses, we find that there has been a deliberate pattern of foreshadowing which should frighten anyone who has been trifling with God's mercy. The One who made the earth, who intended its bright witnesses to sing to him and to us, can just as easily return it to its initial formlessness.

The Chaos Monster

The ancient near eastern world understood all too well the threat that their environment had the potential to become unglued, to sink into a chaotic morass. Babylonian mythology, for example, envisioned a deity—Tiamat, goddess of the threatening seas—who had the power to bring uncreation upon the earth. In effect, she was the chaos monster who had to be overthrown to prevent her from turning the world into a shapeless ooze.

The Israelites, of course, rejected such mythological notions. The world was not controlled by gods and spirits but by the Creator alone. Yet the children of God were well aware of the religious ideas of their neighbors. Thus the Old Testament Scriptures used elements of ancient near eastern mythology as a sort of apologetic to explain the superiority of Yahweh, who triumphed over all real and imagined powers.

In this context, *the deep (tehom)* in Genesis 1:2 may be important. Many scholars argue that there is a linguistic connection between this Hebrew word and "Tiamat," the chaos monster, so that the act of creation needs to be seen as God's work of pushing back the chaos so that a world of order could be formed and preserved.[1]

This theme is repeated often in the Old Testament in two basic ways. First, chaos (uncreation) is often seen as a mythological monster described by such names as "Rahab" and "Leviathan." God attacks this beast and conquers its power (Job 26:12; Isaiah 27:1). Second, there is the imagery of the seas raging in a stormy attempt to overwhelm the dry land (Jeremiah 5:22; Ezekiel 32:2-8). At times, as in the mythology of the day, the two themes are combined (for example, Isaiah 51:9-10).

The clear teaching of such passages is that no matter what "monsters" of uncreation may lurk at the edges of society, threatening to turn order back into the chaos from which it came, God has set their boundaries, which they cannot cross at will. As Psalm 104:5-9 expresses it:

> He set the earth on its foundations;
> > it can never be moved.
> You covered it with the deep as with a garment;
> > the waters stood above the mountains.
> But at your rebuke the waters fled,
> > at the sound of your thunder
> > > they took to flight;
> > they flowed over the mountains,
> they went down into the valleys,
> > to the place you assigned for them.
> You set a boundary they cannot cross;
> > never again will they cover the earth.

Yet the forces of chaos have not been destroyed so that

they cease to be a threat. They are *held back* by the God who sustains the world. There is a disturbing potential for them to break free, if only God would lift the heavy hand he has placed upon them.

This, many in Israel believed, could never happen, for if anything distinguished God's people from their neighbors, it was the security they had in the nurturing and protecting God. Such appears to have been the reasoning of the majority of Israelites. We read, for example, in Jeremiah 7 that the inhabitants of Jerusalem were certain that God would never allow his holy city to be destroyed by invaders, no matter how evil his people were.

But they were wrong, even as the inhabitants of the earth in Noah's day were wrong, for chaos was only to be held in check as long as God was determined to do so. Because his promises of nurture and protection were conditional, depending on the obedience of people of Israel, there were no absolute guarantees.

The Great Flood

There are many debates about the meaning and extent of the Flood in the time of Noah, but for our purposes we need to focus on just one element—here we see the dark witnesses in full uniform, doing the task for which they were made.

The people of the earth in Noah's time had fallen into a rebellion from which they had no desire nor will to escape. The sin of each generation became a landing for the construction of staircases to greater depths. Soon every movement of every heart plotted only evil, never good (Genesis 6:5).

In this context, humanity could not hope to observe the bright witnesses in creation—glory and nurture—with anything even approaching true insight. Most people were blind and deaf and dumb and senseless. Nothing could reach them any longer, and thus God determined to doom them all.

We must remind ourselves here that the dark witnesses of nature—penalty and precariousness—as embodied in the Flood which was to come, were not merely hammers of final judgment. Because Noah and his family found grace in the eyes of God and were to be preserved, penalty and precariousness were not simply to be the epitaphs of the doomed, but severe lessons to the saved. They were intended to leave a legacy to the survivors, a message to be spoken with dread to one's children.

In the flood we find the dark witnesses uniting into a warning of coming final uncreation. God's first warning was the most severe signal man has yet received. At least two lines of evidence support the view that God was saying through the flood, "I who made the world and nurtured it, can just as easily return it to its formlessness."

First, we have God's own announcement of his plan to bring the waters upon humanity: "I will wipe mankind, whom I have created, from the face of the earth—men and animals, and creatures that move along the ground, and birds of the air—for I am grieved that I have made them" (Genesis 6:7).

Notice here the direct reference to the fact that God had created what he was now destroying. Notice as well that the list of the earth's inhabitants is given in virtually the reverse order to that in Genesis 1 (except for the ground creatures and birds which were created on the same day). By reversing the order, God was emphasizing that the act of creation would be reversed, that nature would be unmade.

The second evidence for the flood as a sign of uncreation comes from Genesis 7:11: "In the six hundredth year of Noah's life, on the seventeenth day of the second month—on that day all the springs of the great deep burst forth, and the floodgates of the heavens were opened."

The key word here is *deep (tehom)*, the term from Genesis 1:2, which has possible linguistic associations with the Babylonian notion of Tiamat, the chaos monster. While Scripture is not here sinking into mythology, a statement was being made that the chaotic waters, so feared by ancient peoples that they created myths about them, were no longer to be held back.[2] Even without a direct knowledge of the Tiamat story, the early reader of Genesis would have understood that "the deep" was linked to chaos, for in Genesis 1:2 the term lies in virtual parallel with "formless and empty."

The great flood was a statement and a prophecy. Just as sin is mirrored in damage to the earth, so the end of the patience of God will mean uncreation, an end to the existence of the world blighted by fallen humanity. This is the ultimate testimony of the dark witnesses of penalty and precariousness. In the homes of the descendants of Noah, the story was to be told with quiet awe. The God who made the earth can unmake it if that is his will. No one was to be deceived by the predominance of bright witnesses, for one divine catastrophe would be enough to undo everything.

Scorched Earth

The life of ancient near eastern peoples was a harsh one in which wars among the numerous small kingdoms raged constantly. Israel's security in God, as long as she did not sin, needs to be seen in the context of the sort of ferocious conflict which was the common experience of other nations. When Israel failed her Maker, she too came under the precariousness of invasion and battle.

Ancient warfare was a horrible yet fascinating phenomenon. The goal of an invading army was not generally to subdue an enemy as much as it was to cripple its foe. This was especially true when the adversary had been a thorn in one's side for many years. Thus it was considered perfectly logical and right to see an enemy as defeated only when the necessities for his very survival had been destroyed. It is not surprising, in this context, that warfare became a metaphor for God's warning about a coming uncreation of the earth.

The Bible reveals a number of details about the scorched earth policy so common to ancient conflict. A classic example is Israel's attack on sinful Moab. God's command to the Israelites was clear: "You will overthrow every fortified city and every major town. You will cut down every good tree, stop up all the springs, and ruin every good field with stones" (2 Kings 3:19). Israel did just that. "They destroyed the towns, and each man threw a stone on every good field until it was covered. They stopped up all the springs, and cut down every good tree" (2 Kings 3:25a).

It would be easy to be sidetracked into questioning why God, the wise ecologist, would command such devastation. Our study of the dark witnesses should show us that God's action here was simply a statement of penalty and precariousness against a nation which had moved beyond his patience. Israel was an instrument of the divine will on a single occasion. This was not a mandate to join God in destroying the world in general.

It is with the actual procedures of scorched earth that the metaphor takes on its true role. The idea of scorched earth related to the common practice of burning up everything that was conquered, as in Babylon's last invasion of Judah (2 Kings 25:9-10). While invading nations often sought to preserve portions of the economy which could be exploited, punishment for breaches of covenant or rebellion generally resulted in destruction. Beyond fire, salt was often sprinkled on conquered land (Judges 9:45; Psalm 107:33-34; Zephaniah 2:9).[3] Gaster is surely correct when he argues that this was a "symbol of devastation." Salt alone damaged the topsoil (though deeper sowing actually promoted growth), but combination of salt with other substances such as sulfur guaranteed barren land where crops had once flourished (see Deuteronomy 29:23).[4]

It is in this context that the most frightening warnings of uncreation had their place, for scorched earth became a metaphor for a world unmade. Michael De Roche, a Canadian scholar, has written extensively on the uncreation theme. He shows that the imagery of total war, such as that in Zephaniah 1:2-3a, has become something more than a temporal description:

> "I will sweep away everything
> from the face of the earth,"
> > declares the LORD.
> "I will sweep away both men and animals;
> I will sweep away the birds of the air
> and the fish of the sea."

The terminology "from the face of the earth" recalls the statement repeated in descriptions of the Great Flood (Genesis 6:7; 7:4; 8:8). Even more significantly, all creation is involved in the judgment. Once again, as in Genesis 6:7, each creature group is named in reverse order to that of Genesis 1. Creation is being reversed, unmade, uncreated.[5]

Similarly, Hosea 4:1-3 shows the same sort of reverse order in describing the downfall of the inhabitants of the earth.[6]

The most chilling of all the references to scorched earth as a metaphor for uncreation, however, has to be Jeremiah 4:23-26, introduced earlier in the preface of this book. The imagery could be seen as mere poetic license to emphasize the threat of the Babylonians. But the reader cannot escape the more cosmic allusions to "formless and empty" (4:23, the same words as in Genesis 1:2), disappearance of the heavenly lights (4:23), absence of people (4:25), departure of the birds (4:25), and the description of the fruitful land as a "desert" (4:26).

What is the meaning of such passages, and what are they warning us about in our current ecological crisis? First, we are reading about dark witnesses—penalty and precariousness—which have combined into uncreation as the result of human sin. God announced to Judah in Jeremiah 4:18a: "Your own conduct and actions have brought this upon you."

Second, the dark witnesses can operate directly under the control of God, as in the natural disaster of the Great Flood, or he can place the power of environmental doom in the hands of human beings who act as his instruments. The devastation brought about in Judah by an invading Babylon or in Moab by angry Israelites was human activity which executed the judgment of God by bringing ecological disaster.

What we have discovered, in effect, is that the dark witnesses need not be lightning bolts from heaven, nor earthquakes, nor floods. They can be put into place by human beings who, out of sin or ignorance, become unwitting instruments of God's severe warning to a humanity gone wrong. Notice, however, that this does not condone the perpetrators. Though God used Babylon, that nation remained under his constant judgment for its rapacious quest for territory which was not its own (Jeremiah 50-52).

The importance of the uncreation theme lies in its cosmic nature. It is not limited to one small nation in past time. Rather, it is projected onto the whole earth and relates to our present and future. How close we are to the time of the uncreation of the earth is not a knowledge given to mere mortals. But it is significant that the warnings of ecologists, related to the very real potential that we will wipe out life on this planet through pollution, is very close to the uncreation theme of Scripture.

Is it possible that the emerging ecological nightmare is part of God's final call to a humanity which has ignored every witness of creation already given? Could it be that we who, for whatever reason, have muddied our own stream and are dying of thirst, are receiving a final dose of God's grace as he calls out through man-made dark witnesses, "Return to me"? What an irony it would be if we ourselves became the instruments of uncreation.

Racing Toward the End

It is in the eschatological passages of Scripture, those relating to the end of time, that we find the fruition of all of God's warnings about uncreation. Before we move into that realm, let us remind ourselves again that God's intention all along has been restoration of the world he made. It will be all too easy, as we move into the gloom of the earth's future, to forget that God's plan was to enhance the bright witnesses. If we are to believe the Bible's declarations of the Creator's sovereignty, his original intention will ultimately triumph, no matter how dark the times may become in the interim.

When Jesus spoke to his disciples about the time of the end (Matthew 24-25), the topic was not new to them. Nor was it unusual to link the last days with strange disturbances in nature. God through Joel had announced:

> "I will show wonders in the heavens
>   and on the earth,
>   blood and fire and billows of smoke.
> The sun will be turned to darkness
>   and the moon to blood
>   before the coming of the great and
>   dreadful day of the Lord." (Joel 2:30-31)

Zechariah 14:1-4 prophesied that the Mount of Olives would be split in two on the Day of the Lord. Ezekiel 38 presented an apocalyptic nightmare consisting of a great earthquake followed by rain, hail, and burning brimstone from the skies (38:19-22). Isaiah 13:9-10 saw the Day of the Lord as time of barren land and darkened stars.

Such imagery formed the background of Jesus' significant prophecies about the last days. Of particular importance is Jesus' response to the question: "What will be the sign of your coming and of the end of the age?" (Matthew 24:3). He began by pointing to three types of phenomena which would act as signs: warfare, earthquakes, and famines. The first of these is easily understood, since an increase in warfare and in the wickedness of the last times obviously go together.

But earthquakes and famines do not appear to have the same link to sin unless we see them as dark witnesses. Then they make frightening sense—the end is the time of uncreation, when penalty and precariousness will increase markedly. These natural disasters will be the rumblings of a greater catastrophe to come.

The signs of earthquake and famine are not in themselves

announcements that the end has arrived. Rather, they are warnings that action must be taken because God is concluding his dealings with this present world. The warnings will increase as the last hour draws nearer. Jesus described them as "the beginning of birth pains" (Matthew 24:8), signals that greater pain is to come and that something must be done before it is too late to act.

When the end comes, it will be immediately preceded by a shaking of the entire physical universe. By that time, however, there will be little opportunity to make things right with God.

With the books of 2 Peter and Revelation, we are left in no doubt that the uncreation of the earth, brought about by willful sin, is inevitable. Revelation 16, a litany of horror, spells out the death-throes of our planet: The waters of the earth will turn to blood and everything in the sea will die (16:3-6); the sun will scorch the people of the earth with intense heat (16:8-9); finally an earthquake, such as no one has ever seen, will shatter the world and will be followed by hailstones of immense size (16:18-19).

Then, according to 2 Peter 3:7, 10-12, as if our battered earth could take no more, the uncreation will be completed in one burst of searing flames. Then the process will be done, for the same word by which God once flooded the earth (as a warning) will one day call fire down upon it (2 Peter 3:5-7). Nothing will be left but the matter from which it came. The planet will die.

The earth is a mirror of human experience. We who have had every bright witness we could ever hope for, have chosen the darkness. Finally, one day, there will be no way to avert the catastrophe.

Could our ecological crisis have a role to play in the events of the end? Certainly pollution is an element of uncreation. We are killing the earth's ability to support life. While there are risks in speculating, it is significant that many of the phenomena of the last days could as easily be the result of our ecological actions as the direct work of God.

Most of us who live in cities have already seen a blood-red moon on a smoggy night (Joel 2:31). The death of all life in our seas is today no longer the wild dream of some science fiction writer (Revelation 16:3-6). The greenhouse effect and the rapid diminishing of the ozone layer could bring scorching heat to the earth (Revelation 16:8-9). Even the immense earthquake and hailstones of Revelation 16:18-19 could be brought about by a global nuclear war followed by a "nuclear winter."

Whether or not we can make such connections, we must be aware that our attack on the earth God gave us *is of the same order as natural disasters and other phenomena which are the work of the dark witnesses.* The world is being unmade, and our ecological viciousness is part of the process. Let us not think that God would never allow us to wipe ourselves out with our own pollution. This may be exactly the means he uses to end the time of his grace and patience.

What an irony that would be that we, the brave new people of a brave new age, would use our accomplishments to bring about our own demise. Could we then raise our fists against our Maker and say, "Why did you refuse to save us?" Or would we have to admit that God has done everything in his vineyard to make it flourish, only to have us break down its vines, push over its towers, and shatter its cisterns?

The Glorious Triumph of the Sovereign God

It does not end here, with humanity standing aghast as the world collapses and burns. God's plans for the world cannot be dashed so easily. Nothing we have done or will do can prevent him from carrying them out.

The end, surprisingly, is not tragedy, but a return to glory. We should have seen that already in our human experience with God. The gospel message of salvation in Christ embodies the key to a proper understanding of the way in which death and destruction can bring life. We see it in Jesus, who introduced resurrection into our fallen experience.

In the spiritual realm, salvation means a necessary death with Christ if we are to have any hope that we will live with him. We are crucified spiritually with him and resurrected with him. As Colossians 3:3 so simply puts it: "For you died, and your life is now hidden with Christ in God."

While there are exceptions, such as Enoch, Elijah, and believers who will be alive when the Lord returns, most human beings will experience physical death as well, whether they are Christians or not. Physical death is a necessity if we are ever truly to come to life (1 Corinthians 15:36).

The principle may be summarized as follows: *Everything touched by sin normally must die and be reborn before it is fit to remain eternally in the presence of God.*

Death in such a context is not meaningless. It is the final purge before the true life-giving purposes of God can be achieved. This is the message of Romans 8:18-25: Creation has groaned under the curse for these many centuries, not because it has been doomed forever, but because it has been awaiting redemption. The freedom in which nature will one day rejoice is the freedom of believers in Christ—a liberty one receives only by death to the bondage of sin and new life in Christ (v. 21).

Our world has been blighted by the Fall, attacked by

dark witnesses, and ravaged by the waste products of our striving for a man-made Utopia. If our planet is ever, ultimately, to be what God intended when he first declared it good, it has to die and become a new creation. Nothing less can purge it of its corruption.

Finally, in the destiny of creation, we see the victory of the Maker. He has not been thwarted from his intention to make the bright witnesses—glory and nurture—blaze with light. One day, all creation will sing to him as it did when he first formed it. And the dark witnesses will vanish forever.

In that day, the vision of John on the island of Patmos will have its fruition:

> Then I saw a new heaven and a new earth, for the first heaven and the first earth had passed away, and there was no longer any sea. I saw the Holy City, the new Jerusalem, coming down out of heaven from God, prepared as a bride beautifully dressed for her husband. And I heard a loud voice from the throne saying, "Now the dwelling of God is with men, and he will live with them. They will be his people, and God himself will be with them and be their God. He will wipe every tear from their eyes. There will be no more death or mourning or crying or pain, for the old order of things has passed away." (Revelation 21:1-4)

In the remade world, the sea, that terrible symbol of uncreation, will be gone. The pain of living among dark witnesses will be eliminated. No longer will there be fear, for our security will be made perfect in him. Then the Garden of Eden will be reborn (Revelation 22). At its center will be the tree of life, available to all the redeemed so that they might eat and be healed (22:2, 14).

And God will make all things new.

Notes

1. In this regard, see the balanced argument of "Deep; Deeps; Depths," *International Standard Bible Encyclopedia*, 1 (Grand Rapids: Wm. B. Eerdmans Publishing Co., 1979), 910.

2. See Bruce C. Birch, "Nature, Humanity, and Biblical Theology: Observations Toward a Relational Theology of Nature," *Ecology and Life*, by Wesley Granberg-Michaelson (Waco, Tex.: Word Books, 1988), 147.

3. See ancient near eastern examples in Theodor H. Gaster, *Myth, Legend and Custom in the Old Testament* (New York: Harper, 1969), 428.

4. Ibid., 429-30.

5. Michael De Roche, "Zephaniah 1:2-3: The Sweeping of Creation," *Vetus Testamentum*, 30 (1980): 104-9.

6. Michael De Roche, "The Reversal of Creation in Hosea," *Vetus Testamentum*, 31 (1981): 400-409; compare his "Contra Creation, Covenant, and Conquest (Jer. viii 13)," *Vetus Testamentum*, 30 (1980): 280-90. It is also of interest that Isaiah 30:6-7 describes threatening Egypt as Rahab, the chaos monster (see also Ezekiel 29:3-5; 32:2-8). Invading nations are often described as raging seas (for example, Isaiah 17:12-14), another metaphor for chaos.

6

Creation in Our Hands

When I was nine or ten, my family bought a dog, a rather over-eager German shepherd pup we named Laddie. Being the oldest child, I considered Laddie my own. But the dog had a problem. He believed himself to be the fierce protector of his adoptive family and sought to attack anyone who came near us.

That trait, plus his joy in knocking over garbage cans, brought a stern pronouncement from my father. The dog had to go. Unless my brothers and I could do something with Laddie, he would be sold.

I lost hope. There was nothing that could be done with the foolish beast, and so I withdrew myself from him, knowing that our relationship was doomed. The day the new owner took Laddie away will always remain in my memory, not so much because of my sorrow as because I knew I would always wonder if I could have done something to turn the situation around.

The earth is doomed to destruction. The Bible makes that very plain. It will be burned up and remade to fit the purpose God had for the first creation before our evil was projected on it and it fell under bondage. God has done what was necessary to save his vineyard, but we are turning it into a barren quagmire.

Is there any point in trying to save what is essentially a doomed relationship with our planet? We understand that the proclamation of the gospel will result in the salvation of people. But is the salvation of the earth even remotely a mandate as we race toward the end of time?

There are three possible responses we might make to the ecological crisis: indifference, damaging exploitation, and support for the environment. Each needs serious consideration, for each has been proposed either explicitly or implicitly.

Indifference

The option of indifference seems to be the evangelical response of choice. I say that not with sarcasm but with sorrow. The simple fact is that the evangelical response to our crumbling environment has been a stunning silence.

Christian magazines seldom even mention ecology, let alone provide a biblical perspective on the crisis facing our world. Woe betide the evangelical pastor who devotes a sermon to the Christian's responsibility to nature. Such a man would surely be labeled a victim of creeping liberalism.

Evangelicals are unconcerned about the fate of the earth, at least as far as the evidences of church life and Christian literature indicate. This is amazing on two counts: First, Christians appear to be ecstatic about nature. We have proliferated summer camps; our hymns are filled with praise to God for "rocks and trees and skies and seas";

and we are always searching for more refreshing spots for weekend retreats. Second, it is difficult to understand how Christians can miss the ecological crisis that is screaming at us. It is a top priority of both the American and Canadian governments. Secular magazines such as *Time* and *National Geographic* have devoted cover stories to it.

We are left with something that is less a tragic reality than a shocking one. To quote David Douglas: "As stewards of creation, we have often dozed in the pews."[1] Ecology, despite our love of nature, is for us a secular topic, unspiritual, and thus to be relegated to others who are "into that sort of thing."

If this is truly our response to the disaster awaiting our planet, it is an error of immense proportions. Not only have we forgotten that this world was made by God, not only have we ignored the only mandate he ever gave us concerning it—to *tend* the Garden—but we have missed the entire theological import of creation as something formed to give God glory.

Perhaps it is our spiritual tradition, with its emphasis on higher values and its wariness of the physical, that has led us down the wrong path. We have trained ourselves to deny the appetites of the flesh and to avoid the entrapments of this life—wealth, security, pleasure. All of these have strong ties with matter, and thus we have unconsciously labeled the physical as evil and something to be denied.

Yet, no position could be more unbiblical. It was God who created matter. The physical world did not become evil in itself even after the Fall. In fact, the physical is foundational, not just to this life but to our heavenly existence. We, like Christ, will be raised with physical bodies (1 Corinthians 15). As well, the new heavens and the new earth of Revelation 21 appear to have all the properties of matter.

Indifference will not do, as comfortable and even as pious as it may seem. We live with physical bodies in a physical world, and we simply cannot deny that reality. No matter how much we may seek a spiritual existence, the physical is always there. The tangible creation cannot be ignored.

Damaging Exploitation

The theological institution with which I am involved is planning for relocation. The existing buildings will be demolished to make way for redevelopment. With the consciousness that we are working within a doomed facility, there is already a strong temptation to neglect it. As we come closer to moving day there will probably be an increasing edge to our carelessness until some of us will actually make light of inflicting real damage on it.

Christians, as we saw in the first chapter, have been accused by Lynn White and others of being the source of the current ecological crisis. It is said that we understand the Bible to be urging us to exploit this temporal world simply because it is temporal, a stage on the way to a more permanent heaven. With a consciousness that uncreation awaits as the final step, we are said to have all the ammunition necessary to become enemies of the earth.[2]

To anyone who truly grasps the meaning of Christianity, such a charge seems ludicrous. I have never met any Christian who seriously argued: "This world is doomed anyway, so I might as well get everything I can out of it regardless of the damage I do."

Common sense tells us that damaging exploitation of our world is simply not an option to be entertained. First, the environment still reflects the glory and nurture of God. To the extent that I damage it, these witnesses are diminished. Second, the earth is the Lord's, given to us in trust. His one and only mandate for us is to *tend* the garden. We have in no sense been given permission to participate in God's uncreating judgment. Third, creation must still nurture us and our children. It is insane to shoot the horse you are riding.

Fourth, and perhaps most significant for us, to abuse creation is to be part of the pattern of sin. We have looked at four witnesses in creation, two of them bright and two of them dark. The dark witnesses are intruders which exist solely because of human sinfulness. They work in the sphere of damage to the environment. To join the ecological exploiters is to align ourselves with lost humanity rather than the living Christ.

Those who pollute the earth have taken on a role which is an evil counterpart to the proper work of God. John Carmody writes:

> When one turns to Jesus and starts to view the world as a gift of Jesus' Father's love, the sins of human beings against the world . . . stand out in bolder relief. Then our ecological depredations take on the lineaments of an egocentric denial of God. Were God in his heavens, we would not so pollute the skies. . . . The ruin of nature and the denial of God go hand in hand, because both overexalt human beings.[3]

There is a label for such actions based on such an attitude. It is *sin*. To pollute our world is *sinful*, not because it turns beauty to ugliness but because it makes us illegitimate gods defiantly attacking what was made by Another, who still claims ownership over it.

Only the Creator can unmake what he has formed. Our sinfulness tells us we can do what we want with God's creation, as if we had made it ourselves. Our sinfulness causes us to use our own accomplishments to bring out the dark witnesses which will eventually destroy our environment. Our sinfulness will eventually destroy our environment. Our sinfulness is mirrored in the earth: If we were holy, we would still be in Eden.

For a Christian even to consider damaging the earth because it is doomed anyway is to sink to the depths of evil folly. Ecological trauma, no matter what its actual cause, is a manifestation of human sin, an echo of the depravity of our souls. We dare not have any part in it.

Active Support

We have used up our options. Indifference will not do, nor will damaging exploitation. All that is left is active support, a return to the command to tend the garden and make it flourish.

Even as we come, perhaps slowly, to that conclusion, we begin to see how much of a problem it will be for us. Where do we start? How can a few Christians, with a theology that says we must care for the earth, hope to do anything to stave off the attacks on creation by big industry and over-populated society? Is nature actually "in our hands" as the chapter title suggests, or have we lost our power to have any influence over its fate?

In order to answer these questions and to assess our possible influence in our polluted world, let us first investigate the problems which brought humanity into its current crisis. Beyond ignorance of what we have been doing to our environment (a problem which is solving itself as the crisis grows) we may identify two other key factors—economics and inertia.

Economics. Pollution and economic development go together. This is not a new insight. We can go back to the time of Solomon and observe the way the upwardly mobile people of the ancient near east decimated the forests of Lebanon as part of a growth industry from which even Israel benefited. The same sort of environmental destruction occurred in the forests of ancient China as its economy expanded. Throughout history, the exploitation of economic opportunities has brought about the exploitation of nature.

In our time, capitalism has often been seen as public enemy number one of the ecological crisis. Some have argued that the capitalist emphasis on profit and competition demands that expensive environmental safeguards will be avoided unless strictly enforced by law.

Much as we might hope for a simple scapegoat, the problem cannot be laid at the door of capitalism alone. The fact that scientists in Communist China are now issuing dire warnings of their own impending environmental disaster shows that pollution is not a problem created by only one type of economic system. Now that the Eastern bloc countries have rejected communism, the West has begun to learn of the horrifying ecological damage these countries now have to attempt to repair.[4] The real issue is not the method by which an economy structures itself as much as it is the goal of that economy. It is here that capitalism and communism come to a strange meeting of minds, for both emphasize *growth.*

The twentieth century concept of growth is two-sided. For the producer, the plan is to develop an ever-increasing variety and quantity of goods while ensuring that new markets for those goods are constantly being opened. For the consumer, the goal is a better life style which necessarily includes an increased variety and quantity of material possessions.

This perhaps simplistic description of current growth economies appears to lie at the heart of the philosophies of most societies on earth. We all want to technologize, to grow richer in every way, to share in the good life.

Growth is not necessarily an evil thing. We need it to support increases in population and to remove inequities in the economic life of society. Many argue that industry requires growth simply to guarantee sufficient stability in the marketplace.[5]

Unfortunately, a growth/consumerism mentality, when it moves beyond a basic and necessary level, clashes with proper care of the earth. This is true for one reason: the earth is capable of supporting only a limited amount of growth. If we move too fast, we quickly deplete our natural resources and begin pouring more pollutants into the environment than the earth can scrub out.

An honest look at twentieth century life tells us that we have developed a vision of Utopia which is beyond the earth's ability to realize. We are gobbling up our resources and poisoning our skies, seas, and ground, all because we have come to believe that our consumer life-style is necessary.

This is not just a North American problem nor a European problem. It is a problem in Brazil and Nigeria and China and Bora-Bora. Humanity has developed an ethic which sees growth, production, and advancement as the true goal of man. The Kenyans, for example, in March 1989 declared that they would *increase* the production of CFC chemicals which damage the ozone layer. Their argument: Such chemicals are vital to industrialization; if the West wants their use to disappear, scientists of the West will have to create viable alternatives.[6]

Critics of the sorts of economic goals that place material advancement ahead of care for the earth are beginning to call for a reevaluation of our true needs as opposed to our clamoring wants. John Carmody writes:

> It's hard to imagine the United States . . . shifting from a consumerist ethic to an ethic stressing genuine needs. That would be like a junkie going cold turkey, an alcoholic staying on the wagon. . . . Millions have bought a terrible bill of goods, star-studded with the premise that money and possessions will make them happy. The dream was bound to turn nightmarish.[7]

And Douglas Hall asks:

> Is the quality of our life dependent on confronting in our supermarket, whole aisles filled with soaps and cleaning fluids bearing a hundred different brand names—products whose manufacture and use are polluting whole waterways and killing off ancient forms of life?[8]

The problem is one of attitude. We have evolved a hazardous mind-set which can be described only as covetousness—the desire to have more than our earth can give us. Our legitimate search for security and freedom from want has become illegitimate all too quickly.

Here nature serves as a valuable but usually ignored indicator of our encroaching greed: Nature suffers when we move beyond our God-given boundaries. If what we feel compelled to do requires us to damage the earth, then it is time for us to question our motives and assess our supposed needs. We must never forget that the earth acts as a mirror of our inner life. When we see dark witnesses forming in the shape of nature's diminished glory and its depleted power to nurture us, we are looking at the reflection of a growing problem in our hearts. Given the polluted state of our planet, it appears that growth/consumer economies are often fueled by desires which God can only call unholy.

Inertia. A man falls to the sidewalk, and we watch with a vicarious embarrassment, waiting for him to get up. But he doesn't move, and we go through a strange process in which normal routine transforms itself into crisis. Ultimately we draw on reserves we were unaware of and call an ambulance, wrap a coat around the fallen man, try to administer first aid.

The movement from life as usual to recognition of a dawning emergency is not an easy one. None of us wants to be thrust without warning into a role that places screaming demands on our deepest resources and moves us into the front lines of life.

We prefer the routine inertia that expects the expected and avoids crises. We do not want yet another problem to burst into the social scene and call for our urgent attention. But when the dawning emergency is the pollution of God's earth, our inertia can easily become a dangerous enemy. Wesley Granberg-Michaelson writes:

> Clearly the Christian community has forgotten its God-given task to "tend the garden." Commitment to preserving God's creation has been nearly non-existent, and often viewed as heretical or irrelevant by many sectors of the church. This has been true particularly for the evangelical community.[9]

We are doing very little about the environment because we have not yet awakened to the realization that there is a crisis before us and that this crisis matters to believers. It is as if we have just seen the man fall to the sidewalk and are still waiting for him to get up. We have not yet grasped that he is not going to get up, that he is in trouble and may die unless we take action.

Ecology is a Christian responsibility, but we Christians remain by-standers, hoping that no one will call on us to get involved to save the earth. Church history shows that there have been many parallels in which inertia took overly long to be overridden: the slave trade, child labor, racial segregation. In every case, it was at first far easier to rest in the chrysalis of inertia than to come to the realization that the problem required a Christian voice. What will it take to break apart our inertia about the environment? Sociologists would tell us that only a complete reversal of mind-set will do the task.

Let's consider an example of the sort of process required. When I was a teenager and refused to accept a cigarette, I was labeled one of those religious types who did not belong to the "in" group. You see, most of my peers could see no earthly reason not to smoke. Most people did. It was the accepted thing.

Then the anti-smoking campaigns began. Medical people warned of severe risks to health, though at first they were ignored. What appears to have finally turned the tide was a series of advertisements by movie stars and other prominent people proclaiming that smoking is a filthy habit. We all remember the sorts of statements that were made: "Kissing a smoker is like kissing an ashtray."

Smoking gradually became uncool. It became a vicious habit which people felt a strange new compulsion to break. Smokers were banned from lighting up in airplanes and buses and public buildings. Tobacco companies began waging strident counter-campaigns to win back support, only to find that their sales dropped year after year.

What happened? The mind-set of North Americans shifted. What had once been viewed as good, pleasurable, and relaxing became objectionable and crude. Just as fashions change, so the mind-set of society about smoking had been altered.

In our time, the evangelical consensus on ecology has been, "Leave it to the ecologists. This is not a spiritual issue." This consensus, this mind-set, however, is wrong. Evangelicals have missed the point that the earth is the Lord's and the things that happen to it mirror the heart condition of the people who inhabit it. Just as society's opinion about smoking required a shift in mind-set, so evangelicals desperately need a new consciousness about the environment.

How do we break out of the inertia and change our collective mind about the ecological crisis? We do it by confronting the message of the Scriptures head on and admitting that we have been wrong. If the Bible is truly our supreme rule of faith and practice, then it should now be speaking to us with a voice that cannot be denied—to ignore the earth and to be uninvolved in its care is wrong. It is sin. It requires repentance.

Breaking free of inertia demands effort, for repentance is not a painless process. But we are no strangers to changing our minds. Salvation has already demanded of us an entire change of heart. In Christ, in the wisdom of his word, we have both the reasons and the power to challenge our previous false assumptions and to get involved in defending the earth from the crushing onslaught of the dark witnesses of environmental destruction.

The Search for Moral Direction

In chapter 1, we cited an important statement from Louis Moncrief that the first obstacle to beating the ecological crisis is "an absence of personal moral direction concerning our treatment of our natural resources."[10]

If believers in Christ are now to change their mind-set about their long-standing indifference to the environment's problems, then we should be able to articulate such a "moral direction," for that is supposed to be one of the things we do best. There must be some biblical rationale we could verbalize to a society that sees little reason to get off the treadmill of growth and exploitation.

In the midst of such a statement, if we are able to formulate one, perhaps we could discover a fifth witness to provide a resolution for the dilemmas presented by the other four, a witness related to our new life in Christ.

Notes

1. David Douglas, "Wild Country and Wildlife: A Spiritual Preserve," *Christian Century*, 4-11 January 1984, 12.

2. See chapter 1, notes 16 and 18.

3. John Carmody, *Ecology and Religion: Toward a Christian Theology of Nature* (New York: Paulist Press, 1983), 79.

4. See "Darkness at Noon," *Time*, 9 April 1990, 50-57.

5. For a Christian perspective see Walter L. Owensby, *Economics for Prophets: A Primer on Concepts, Realities, and Values in Our Economic System* (Grand Rapids: Wm. B. Eerdmans Publishing Co., 1988), 8-13.

6. One of the best analyses of the problem is K. Nurnburger, "Ecology and Christian Ethics in a Semi-Industrialized and Polarized Society," *Are We Killing God's Earth? Ecology and Theology*, ed. W. S. Vorster (Pretoria: University of South Africa, 1987), 50-53. He argues that producers tend to outstrip the ability of consumers to purchase the goods produced. Thus advertising must be used to convince consumers to buy goods they cannot afford.

In Third World countries, the means to produce processed goods diminishes because First and Second World producers have the finances to produce items of greater quality. Thus Third World economies find they have only two commodities to offer: cheap labor and unprocessed natural resources.

This perpetuates the poverty in such nations so that temptations to abuse the environment (by burning forests to get farmland, for example) are severe. Who cares about tomorrow if one cannot survive today? When western nations call for bans on environmentally damaging practices, nations like Kenya retort: "Who are you to demand that we destroy our potential to industrialize when you have been polluting the earth for decades in your own desire to advance technologically? All you want is to keep us in subservience forever."

7. Carmody, *Ecology and Religion*, 144-45.

8. Douglas John Hall, *Imaging God: Dominion as Stewardship* (Grand Rapids: Wm. B. Eerdmans Publishing Co., 1986), 196.

9. Wesley Granberg-Michaelson, *Ecology and Life: Accepting Our Environmental Responsibility* (Waco, Tex.: Word Books, 1988), 18.

10. See chapter 1, note 22.

Creation Reclaimed

We live in what is often called a post-Christian society. The Judeo-Christian heritage, which once formed the foundation of North American society, is evaporating, at least as far as its power to give direction to life decisions is concerned.

In its place, we now find a wide-ranging tolerance based on the cult of the individual. Each of us is said to have a unique and inalienable identity. Each of us walks to the beat of a different drummer. Thus society tells us that the supreme good is respect for our differences, acceptance of a variety of lifestyles and mind-sets.

This, of course, as evangelicals have been arguing for many years, erodes a consciousness of right and wrong, good and evil. If every viewpoint must be tolerated, then no opinion or assertion is more likely to be true than any other.

When we incorporate such tolerance into the ecological realm, we immediately encounter some serious obstacles to saving the earth. Who is to say that one person's desire to clean up pollution is better than another person's strategy to improve our standard of living, no matter what the cost? We might dismiss this question as foolishness, because everyone knows it is better to preserve the earth. Yet a simple counter-question demonstrates the unstable ground on which we stand: How do we *know* it is better to preserve the earth?

Some argue that self-preservation is a basic human instinct. We care for the earth because we have to live in it. Yet we realize that the things we are doing to our world will probably not kill us, though they may endanger our children. And, try as we might, we are going to have a hard time stirring up the motivation, based on our children's future, to act to beat the crisis in the environment now. There are too many temptations to leave the problem to the next generation when advanced technology will far outstrip our present ability to do the required ecological cleanup.

Christians living in a post-Christian world have a unique opportunity to address the central problem in the environmental crisis—a lack of clear moral direction. We have the anchor that most of the rest of western society has lost. We are guided by an absolute reality, while the majority of our fellow-citizens have only their deadly tolerance to guide them.

And now Christians need to begin to speak. Ron Elsdon has written, "If the Christian faith contains a true and unique revelation of God to man, and if the environmental problems which face us stem from the fallen character of man . . . then our participation is essential."[1] His point must be taken seriously, for the damage mankind is doing to our world has powerful biblical and theological ramifications.

We must begin to communicate a distinctly Christian response to the question: "Why save the earth?" While it may include a call to think of the heritage we are leaving to our children, it must cover far more. Unless it is rooted in solid biblical evidence and is explained in terms compatible with the gospel message, it cannot hope to have the impact it requires.

Before we can move to such a response, we must, however, lay to rest the most popular religious framework in the ecological debate—Pantheism.

Pantheism

A common accusation in our time is that human beings pollute the earth because we consider ourselves superior to the other inhabitants of our planet. We believe it is our right to tamper with the world, to rule it, to exploit it. The key term here is "anthropocentrism," the concept that man is at the center of nature and all creation is for man's use.

There is no doubt that concepts of dominion, of anthropocentrism, have formed an excuse for pollution and other forms of damage to the earth, though, as we saw in chapter 1, the Bible gives no justification for such concepts. But the primary alternative that has been suggested has problems of its own.

In our time, eastern philosophy has become part of the North American psyche. Whether we label it as the New Age Movement or pop-Hinduism or pop-Zen, its basis in pantheism determines its approach. Pantheism argues that all things that exist are totally inter-connected because there is only one essence of which the whole universe is constructed.

If we are to speak of God in such a philosophy, we must say that God is the sum of all that exists; that is, God and the universe are the same. Rather than being above what he has made, God is the essence of which the universe consists. Pantheism argues, therefore, that everything has the essence of deity and nothing can be seen as greater or more important than anything else. Each thing in the universe is a part of the whole, of the same substance and thus of the same value.

Why is pantheism championed within the ecological debate? Simply because it rejects anthropocentrism and the concept of man's right to have dominion over nature. Jackson Ice, for example, the scholar who outdoes Lynn White in condemning Christianity's supposed exploitive tendencies, writes:

> We must strive to become reintegrated with the whole of nature from which we have become estranged. . . . This means, initially, that we must temper our harsher sentiments nurtured by a radical monotheism with the more tender, vivifying, and unifying spirit expressed in pantheistic religions. . . . The less aggressive religions, such as Shinto, Confucianism, Taoism, and the American Indian religions, which teach the harmony of man with Nature and stress noninterference with her sacred ways, perhaps possess the world view now offering the strongest hope for saving mankind from its present dilemma.[2]

Such sentiments are widespread in current ecological articles and books, so much so that pantheism could be called the religion of ecology. On the surface, this belief is attractive. It stresses that we are all part of a whole and thus have no right to force our agenda on a world that has as much intrinsic value as we do. "Harmony" is the key word—human beings in a pantheistic system must live in cooperative communion with nature, because we are made of the same stuff as the animals, the rocks, and the trees.

Even some evangelicals have been attracted by features of the philosophy of pantheism. Wesley Granberg-Michaelson, while by no means a pantheist, has suggested that the pantheistic criticism of western society is essentially correct. Modern culture, he argues, is anthropocentric and illegitimately takes a domineering attitude to creation. He asks us, as well, not to be overly hasty in rejecting eastern views of nature.[3]

Granberg-Michaelson has moved even closer to pantheism in his assertion that creation out of nothing *(creatio ex nihilo)* is never taught in Scripture. Rather, he prefers the concept of "emanation"—that creation is an extension of the very life of God, so that the universe is in some sense an actual part of God, bearing his stamp or essence. While God is still seen as beyond what he has made, in emanation we find pantheism's view that matter and "god" are somehow vitally connected:

> This does not equate the creation with God. But it is a far cry from teachings like *creatio ex nihilo*, which so sever God from creation that the source of the created world remains unknown, and its future appears incidental and unimportant. That hardly provides the grounds for the practice of earthkeeping.[4]

For Granberg-Michaelson, God only has a real stake in this world if nature is an extension of himself, a part of his very essence.

Are such concepts biblical? Should we accept emanation as an explanation of what God has made? Should we go further and become pantheists so that we will have a "moral direction" for our care of the earth? The answer is clearly no on all counts.

First, the Bible *does* teach creation out of nothing. Genesis 1 makes it clear that God spoke and things came into being, not that he formed the earth out of himself (a notion common to other cultures of the Ancient Near East). Hebrews 11:3 provides a commentary on the process of creation: "By faith we understand that the universe was formed at God's command, so that what is seen was not made out of what was visible." While this passage is attacking the Greek view of the eternity of matter (a basic assumption in pantheism), it is also stressing that the things God made did not exist before he made them. They were created out of nothing.

Second, pantheism is totally anti-biblical. Beyond Hebrews 11:3, which explicitly rejects the idea that the world's matter is eternal and thus to be equated with deity, we have the strong teaching of Genesis 1:1 that God existed before the world existed. He cannot be both Creator and creation at the same time.

Third, even if pantheism were true, it would fail utterly as a moral direction for the ecological crisis because it provides no motivation for us actually to care for the earth. If I am of the same essence as the animals or the trees so that I must reject all desires to dominate nature, then I must logically also reject any attempt to care for the creation. Pantheism tells me not to tamper with what is. If I cannot tamper with it, I cannot intervene to save it either. As Francis Schaeffer has expressed it, pantheism pushes "both man and nature down into a bog."[5]

Fourth, pantheism is a "romantic illusion."[6] The plain facts of nature demonstrate that hierarchies exist everywhere, that dominion, not equality, is what makes the world go around. Larger animals feed on smaller ones, and plants are consumed by most species. If it were not for plant and animal life, all human beings on earth would quickly die of starvation.

Ordinary human life makes distinctions all the time. We exterminate mosquitoes but we feed our dogs and cats. We catch fish with barbed hooks but shudder at the thought of anyone doing such a thing to our pets. Pantheism does not work because it is unnatural—it corresponds to nothing at all in the reality of the created order.

Fifth, and perhaps most important, pantheism has no explanation for the dark witnesses in nature and thus no solution to the problem of the way our sin is projected on the earth. Schaeffer commented:

Without categories, there is eventually no reason to distinguish bad nature from good nature. Pantheism leaves us with the Marquis de Sade's dictum, "What is, is right," in morals, and man becomes no more than grass.[7]

We have spent a good deal of time on the pantheistic "solution" to the environmental dilemma. It needs emphasis because it is the dominant non-Christian ecological ethic. The crucial question which now faces us is: Can Christianity do better?

A CHRISTIAN ECOLOGICAL ETHIC: THE HOPE FOR A FIFTH WITNESS

Before the coming of Christ, there was no reason for any permanent hope that a way could be found to fight the dark witnesses here in this life. The earth was filled with people who sat in darkness (Matthew 4:16), who could look forward to nothing but eventual uncreation.

If we are to find a fifth witness, another way for the earth to speak clearly again about God, we will find it only in Christ, the bringer of the light. The fifth witness will have the heart of its meaning in the gospel message of people reborn through the blood of the Son, who paid the penalty in full for our rebellion against the Creator.

The image of rebirth (John 3:3-5) provides a symbol which will point us in the proper direction—toward the possibility of starting over with a clean slate, toward the hope of some measure of restoration. That is key to any proper understanding of the way in which the gospel of Christ can form an ecological ethic.

We have already seen a hint of it in God's description of the promised land, this territory in which he intended to rule his people by covenant love. As we saw in chapter 4, the land of Israel, flowing with milk and honey, was potentially to be a restored Eden. Given the obedience of the Israelites, the covenant blessings would have banished the dark witnesses and have allowed the bright ones to shine as God originally intended.

The failure of Israel in no way can be seen as the end of God's purpose to restore the Garden. One day, when he has finally unmade the world, he will bring Eden back in all its splendor (Revelation 22:1-5, 19), and the dark witnesses will vanish forever.

But we live between the times, not yet free of the negative testimonies in nature, not yet past the day of uncreation. Can the gospel speak to the ecological crisis of today? Is there any means of restoration available to these present heavens and earth?

One proposed answer is an interpretation of 2 Corinthians 5:17 recently popularized by Wesley Granberg-Michaelson. He, as others before him, has challenged the common translation, "Therefore if anyone is in Christ, he is a new creation," and renders the main clause as *"there* is a new creation."[8] That is, with the death and resurrection of Christ, God has inaugurated a plan to restore, not just human beings, but the physical creation as well. Just as Christ's kingdom has broken into this world and is conquering the darkness, so God will transform nature itself. Granberg-Michaelson writes:

> In a time of ecological emergency, the church can offer to the world a hope that is rooted in the power of God to bring new life into all that has been created. And that power has already entered into history; it is amongst us now, working to redeem and reconcile all that is broken so the new creation can be realized.[9]

Strangely, he says nothing at all about God's intention finally to burn up the entire creation (2 Peter 3:10).

Granberg-Michaelson's interpretation of 2 Corinthians 5:17, while possible linguistically, fails on two counts. First, the context indicates that Paul had people, and only people, in mind as he wrote of the new creation. In particular, 5:19 indicates that Paul was not thinking of restoration of the physical earth. When he writes of God "reconciling the world to himself," he means "not counting men's sins against them."

Second, Romans 8:18-25 paints a very different scenario from the overly optimistic idea that God intends to restore the world here and now. Creation has groaned in bondage because it was waiting for our redemption, in which it would share (Romans 8:20-21). But we too groan, even now that we are redeemed, because we await another step in God's saving plan—the final redemption of our bodies (Romans 8:22-23). Thus, in this life we, along with creation, continue to suffer under the dark witnesses. Only when we and nature have passed through death into life will full restoration be possible.

Renewal of the Image

If we cannot find in Scripture a plan by which God intends to restore the earth now through the present inbreaking of Christ's kingdom, then how can we formulate a Christian ethic for dealing with the environment? Should we give up in despair and wait for uncreation?

No. There is another direction we can take—to see the new birth as renewing the command given to Adam and Eve in the Garden before they fell.

The original mandate called human beings to proper obedience to God and to careful tending of the creation he had made. The umbrella symbol for this was the concept of "image." Creation in the image of God meant far more than a similarity to the Maker. "Image" is also a verb; we image God by placing his stamp on creation, by caring for it as he cares for it.

The active form of God's image in man has been damaged severely by the Fall. To look now at humanity in its sin, one can scarcely see mankind demonstrating that the Creator is good and just and merciful and holy. There are traces left of the original role assigned to human creation, but rarely enough so that people in their daily experience can bear a realistic witness to the One who formed them. We look at man but do not really see God.

In salvation, however, we find a transformation, a rebirth that wipes the slate clean and gives the hope of starting again. We need not be surprised that this regeneration and its aftermath are several times described in Scripture as a *renewal of the image.* Once rebels and attackers of all things holy, we have surrendered to the Lordship of the Maker and have begun to image him, living as he would live, as he did live, on earth.

Romans 8:29 sees becoming conformed to the image of Christ as the goal of predestination. Second Corinthians 3:18 argues that believers, *as they reflect Christ's glory*, are being transformed into his likeness, moving into greater glory. Colossians 3:10 puts this renewed image directly into the realm of ethics, linking it to the new self which rejects sin.

But can the phenomenon of a renewal of the image through the new birth be translated also into renewal of the earth so that we can see the transformation of human beings as mirrored by some form of transformation in nature? Several lines of evidence show this to be the case.

First, as we have seen, our sin has been reflected onto the physical world in the form of dark witnesses. The opposite—a growing holiness—should logically work through our new lives to overcome the dark witnesses and allow the bright ones to shine.

Second, Scripture specifically links renewed righteousness to a renewed earth (Isaiah 11:1-9; Hosea 2:18-23). This is perfectly consistent with the blessings and cursings of God's biblical covenant. How we live before the Creator determines the well-being (or lack of it) of nature.

Third, the new birth, by its very characteristics, demands that reborn believers take up the role of imaging God in a new way. Salvation demands restoration, recovering lost ground, returning to the original purposes for which we were made. Bruce Birch writes:

> Unless we see human life lived in a vacuum, redemption must involve nature as well because redemption is precisely God's work to restore

the relationships that have been broken by sin.
That is why new creation is such a helpful image
of God's creative work.[10]

Thus in our salvation, we have an imperative to restore
all the original relationships broken by sin—relationships
with God, with one another, and with the earth. In each
case, God had a plan by which we could live successfully
before him and bring him glory. The mandate to tend the
Garden was intended to glorify God, to demonstrate his
power to nurture us, and to make the earth the kind of
environment that would bountifully support our existence.
A return to God requires that we, once again, make
friends with nature.

THE FIFTH WITNESS: RECLAMATION

We have looked at three reasons why the new birth,
seen as a renewal of the role of imaging the Lord, has
ramifications for the earth: The new birth must contradict
the dark witnesses brought about by sin; Scripture links
righteousness with renewal in nature; and the new birth
demands that we restore our broken relationship with our
environment and return to tending the garden.

In salvation we must recognize that God is reclaiming
what sin had taken for itself. Though the earth must still
go through its final uncreation, there is room now for the
new spiritual witness in our hearts to be echoed in a world
still largely ruled by dark witnesses.

Through the Christian declaration of the gospel, there
is room for a visible sign that God is reclaiming lost territory.
We are able to demonstrate this truth through transformed lives, but we must not neglect the power of the
concrete and visible demonstrations God has made available to us. Nothing speaks as strongly to the human heart

as open and tangible symbols. That is why God raised up dark witnesses against the sinful world—when lost mankind could not understand the darkness in its own heart, it could see in threatening nature the testimony that the Creator was rising in judgment.

We are considering here a *fifth witness,* one which recognizes that the dark witnesses remain in the earth, but that new life is awakening through the crucified and risen Christ. The fifth witness demonstrates, through the tangible work of believers, that even as God is reclaiming human hearts, he has laid claim to the environment in which they live. This demands a new consciousness in the hearts of Christians about the need to care for the earth, to restore it as much as possible, and thus to declare that the earth is the Lord's despite all appearances.

We have a mandate to image God, not just spiritually but physically, for the physical has always served as a mirror of the human heart. If the light is now shining within us where once there was darkness, can we choose any other direction than a determination to make the light shine in our environment as well? This is the fifth witness—*a determined effort on the part of believers to heal the earth, to cease contributing to the dark witnesses, and thus to bear a tangible testimony that God is reclaiming all things lost by the Fall.*

Francis Schaeffer spoke of Christian care of the earth in terms of "substantial healing." We are not hoping for a recovery of Eden here and now, any more than we can realistically expect to become totally holy in this life. But just as the fruit of the Spirit grows within us, covering over barren territory brought about by sin, so we should work for a substantial healing of our scarred earth as it becomes more fruitful under our care.[11]

A commitment to the earth under such a life-principle does not detract from a viable presentation of the gospel. Rather, it demonstrates to skeptical unbelievers that Christ in the human heart is relevant to the world and to the crisis now facing it. We possess a moral direction which demands that we work to save humanity from its course toward ecological suicide. As those around us ask, "Why do you, a Christian bound for heaven, care about the earth?" we can respond, "Because the earth is God's, and through the death and resurrection of Christ, he is reclaiming all life for himself."

Notes

1. Ron Elsdon, *Bent World: A Christian Response to the Environmental Crisis* (Downers Grove, Ill.: InterVarsity Press, 1981), 16.

2. Jackson Lee Ice, "The Ecological Crisis: Radical Monotheism vs. Ethical Pantheism," *Religion in Life*, 44 (1975): 207-8.

3. Wesley Granberg-Michaelson, *Ecology and Life: Accepting Our Environmental Responsibility* (Waco, Tex.: Word Books, 1988), 35-45.

4. Wesley Granberg-Michaelson, "Earthkeeping: A Theology for Global Sanctification," *Sojourners*, October 1982, 23.

5. Francis A. Schaeffer, *Pollution and the Death of Man: The Christian View of Ecology* (Wheaton: Tyndale House Publishers, 1970), 33.

6. An expression from Walter Houston, " 'And Let Them Have Dominion . . .' Biblical Views of Man in Relation to the Environmental Crisis," *Studia Biblica 1978: I*, ed. E. Livingstone (Sheffield: JSOT Press, 1979), 165.

7. Schaeffer, *Polution and the Death of Man*, 33.

8. Granberg-Michaelson, *Ecology and Life*, 98ff.

9. Ibid., 116.

10. Bruce C. Birch, "Nature, Humanity, and Biblical Theology: Observations Toward a Relational Theology of Nature," quoted in ibid., 148.

11. Schaeffer, *Pollution and the Death of Man*, 67ff.

Creation under Care

On March 25, 1989, there was a massive spill of crude oil near Valdez, Alaska. Declared the largest accident of its kind in North American history, the slick spread to over a thousand miles of coastline. Joseph Hazelwood, the captain of the tanker which went aground, had turned the wheel over to the third mate, who was not authorized to take command in those waters. The tanker itself had only a single hull. The construction of double hulled oil carriers, which would minimize the risk of a spill, had been deemed uneconomical.

One year later, Hazelwood was acquitted on a felony count of criminal mischief and misdemeanor counts of intoxication and recklessness. On only one misdemeanor charge was he found guilty: negligent discharge of oil. His sentence was a fifty thousand dollar fine and a thousand hours of cleanup work.

Sadly, this is not the first such disaster on the west coast.

Many have been predicting an accident of this size ever since tanker transport of oil was proposed in the 1960s. It is small comfort to know that they were right.

Why do we do it? Why do we take the kind of risks that frighten even the optimists among us? The simple answer is that we are driven by "necessity." We need that oil. We need it to fuel our industry and our cars and our boats. We need it because progress is inevitable and none of us dares stand in its way.

We are victims of our own successes and slaves of our search for paradise regained. Where once the television set was the sign that we had achieved western nirvana, now only a VCR and a microwave will do. Christians, along with the rest of society, have come to believe the unspoken maxim: A certain amount of damage to the earth is the cost of the lifestyle we require; we dare not sacrifice this lifestyle, because there is nothing else to give life meaning.

BECOMING CHAMPIONS OF THE FIFTH WITNESS

In the last chapter, we looked at the possibility of a fifth witness which creation should now be bearing—the testimony that God is reclaiming his rebellious world for himself. As he has captured the hearts of those who have trusted in Christ, so believers in turn have a mandate to image their Lord, not just in their spiritual lives, but in their treatment of the physical environment in which they live.

We recognize that changing our minds about the way we have handled our earth will require costly effort. But suppose, just for argument's sake, that large numbers of Christians were to become champions of the fifth witness. What would it require in our own lifestyles? How would we be different from those in our society who have labeled the good life a necessity and who resist any change that would threaten their experience of the best that life has to offer?

We would have to begin with three basic attitudinal transformations—a reevaluation of "necessity," a recognition that it is proper for a Christian to be involved in the physical realm, and a willingness to believe that the individual is at the heart of any revolution in society. Let us look at each in turn.

A Fresh Look at "Necessity"

In the 1970s, a number of Christian writers began advocating a reevaluation of western materialism. Believers were confronted with titles such as *The Simple Life, Living More with Less,* and *Enough Is Enough.* All this, of course, was seen as fringe stuff, an offshoot of the hippie movement, shot through with erroneous ideas about the way economies work. If all of us were to abandon the powerful attractions of consumerism, it was argued, society would collapse.

Yet we are now seeing, through the sad experience of the eighties, moving into the nineties, that our consumerism is devouring the earth while failing to guarantee the very economic stability we are looking for. Governments are warning that unlimited growth is bad for us. It creates inflation and breeds recessions. Thus, when the economy grows too rapidly, those who hold the ultimate purse strings in society limit the money supply and drive up interest rates so that we will curb our lusts and decrease our spending. However, they do not want to kill the economy, only inhibit its growth, and so, when our spending slows down, it must be restimulated. We continually ride a roller-coaster where "up" and "down" follow one another with breathtaking but increasingly tedious regularity.

At the heart of the problem is a basically crooked motivation created by the advertisers: What you see is what you want. What you want is what you deserve. What you deserve is what you must have. We are, after all, consumers; and consumers must consume.

But suppose that Christians were to challenge that ethic by evaluating what each of our gadgets costs the environment? We could produce a check list: this much in raw materials needed for the latest trinket we desire, this much in energy to produce it, this much to transport it, and so on. Looked at in this light, we could balance the value to society of the things we produce with their cost in resources and pollution.

Take for example an espresso machine or a waffle iron. What is their ecological cost in comparison with their value to us? What does a VCR cost the earth, or a microwave oven? Such costs are difficult to quantify, but here are some of the factors involved:

1. A percentage of the materials, energy, and environmental damage required to construct the plant that made your VCR or microwave.

2. The nonrenewable materials needed to produce the machine.

3. A percentage of the energy required to make it.

4. The energy used and environmental damage resulting from the transportation of the appliance to your store.

5. The ongoing energy required to use the machine.

6. Damage to the environment from the appliance's ultimate disposal in a landfill site.

Could we survive without these things? Would our self-denial as Christians make a statement about our desire to put the precarious earth ahead of the dreams created by advertisers? Could we return to basic foods which have cost the earth little by way of processing? Could we keep our cars a little longer and drive them a little less, all because we do not want to work undue damage in the earth?

The transformation required here is attitudinal. It calls us to question everything we once believed necessary, until we see necessity through God's eyes as the One who made and wants to preserve his world. Perhaps if Christians could begin leading the way in stabilizing our own greed masquerading as need, the earth would begin to have some rest from humanity's voracious appetites.

The Physical Is Okay

Believers are used to being labeled fanatics by unbelievers. But few of us want to hear people within the family of God charging us with misbegotten zeal. The term *environmentalist* has had bad press among Christians. If we as believers are going to make a difference, if we are going to become environmentalists ourselves, we are going to have to tread where few Christians have ever gone—into a concern for the physical earth, no matter what some fellow Christians may think of us.

We have a rationale available to us—the fifth witness— by which we can explain ourselves. We can demonstrate from the Bible that the physical world not only matters to God but is also the visible mirror of what is going on in human hearts. If we love our God, we must also love the planet he made for us.

But boldness is required. We must take action that will have some Christians wondering why we have become sidetracked from our mission for Christ (not realizing that we have taken it up in a new way). Our stand will require us to begin caring deeply about a realm we once ignored as irrelevant or a potential snare to our spirituality.

You, by Yourself, Are Significant

Doubts arise easily in our hearts. "What can *I* do? Who is going to pay any attention to me?" We do not, however, have to look far to discover that individuals can accomplish a great deal. This is not just a patronizing platitude, for God has always operated on the principle that individuals, empowered by the Spirit, can do the impossible.

The early church, an amalgam of common people, turned the world of its day upside down. Every advance of the gospel in church history was begun by individuals who caught a vision of God's purposes and followed it. Now, as we take up the challenge of the fifth witness, we can be assured that the Creator's power will be applied in corresponding measure to our reliance upon him.

MOVING TOWARD A PLAN

In our time, almost any newspaper or magazine can provide sound suggestions for living responsibly in our environment. We are told to cut down our consumption, purchase ecologically safe goods, use unleaded gas, support government measures to decrease pollution, and so on.

But a plan to promote the fifth witness—God's reclamation of a lost world—must go beyond handy tips to the householder. The goal of ecologically sensitive Christians must include a clear demonstration of our desire to attack the dark witnesses and enhance the bright ones so that, above all, those around us may see the glory of the saving God. The following are some of the principles that will guide us.

Preservation of Ecosystems

An ecosystem is a network of cooperating life-forms which exist in a specific area. The principle which Christians need to follow here is that at least a small percentage of existing natural ecosystems must be preserved intact, with minimal human tampering. In North America we have, in part, provided for this through our park systems which remove tracts of land from industrial and residential development.

What is the rationale for Christians supporting the preservation of "green areas"? At a basic level, such natural ecosystems are good for us. Douglas writes:

> Wild country is not sacrosanct: not everything need be protected. But when so little wilderness remains in a nation, the contemplative gifts it offers—such as silence, solitude and a sense of awe—become worth as much as the marketable commodities that can be extracted.[1]

Besides the spiritual impact of nature, preserving parts of creation intact makes good practical sense. If we as a scientific society want to understand how things work, we must leave some parts of the earth untouched (as much as is possible) so that we can study ecosystems as they are.

But the mandate of the fifth witness goes deeper than this. We need to preserve some ecosystems as we have found them because *an ecosystem in its natural equilibrium is the clearest statement that the bright witnesses can provide to the glory and nurture of God.* This is not to say that the dark witnesses are not also present even in "pristine" nature. But, to the extent to which man intervenes in an ecosystem, he tends to give glory to himself for the result. Only when an ecosystem is left alone to be watched with awe, do we properly see God as the sole guarantor of its life and splendor.

William Dyrness, commenting on the importance of a natural ecosystem, writes: "The universal reaction to such pristine beauty is that one feels close to God. . . . Here, more than any other place, we are sharing in God's own delight in his handiwork."[2]

Evangelicals have generally condemned environmentalists who blockade roads to preserve wilderness areas from loggers or other forms of industry. But, much as we may decry some of their methods, their cause is often just. Natural ecosystems need to be preserved because they form the most visible statement of God's claim on the earth. When you walk in wild country, you know that you have entered God's territory and that you must operate under his terms. Nature untouched is the clearest visible sign we have that God is the Maker and we are responsible to him.

There is a danger here. If we are going to support the preservation of natural ecosystems as a statement that God has reclaimed his world, we are going to have to do more than pay lip service to our ecological concern. Walter Houston has made sarcastic reference to nature reserves as "little areas preserved in amber so that we can get on with our pillage of all the rest."[3] Protecting parcels of natural land is only a beginning.

Decisions about Lifestyle and Development

Human beings need homes to live in. They must consume resources gathered from the earth. To live is to be a polluter. Thus we must recognize that any hope of a pure, totally untouched environment is largely an illusion. We may preserve green areas, but just by being people, we bring a certain amount of stress to most of nature. If we want to have cities and industries and farms and highways, we are going to damage certain parts of the earth, even wiping out former ecosystems and replacing them with concrete, steel, and crops.

This, in itself, is not necessarily an evidence of dark witnesses at work. Within the mandate of God for humanity are included such activities as agriculture, home-building, and mining (Deuteronomy 8:6-18). As Meye has put it, "Human work and efforts toward civilization are a part of the realization of full humanity and should not be automatically counted as an assault against nature."[4] It is also clear that ecosystems are often well able to adapt to the things we do to them. They change, but they still support life.[5]

Sadly, however, our generation has moved far beyond the demands of necessity in making use of the earth. Our twentieth century growth is depleting irreplaceable resources and is poisoning nature beyond its ability to cleanse itself. There is only one conclusion to be made: *We must curb our growth.* We must make what will undoubtedly be painful decisions about the luxuries we treasure.

When I read books and articles which argue that our entire society must diminish its level of development and learn to live with less, I experience a sense of despair. Society will probably do nothing of the kind. It will continue to grow until the earth is strangled by our excesses.

But there is a way to do something at least to limit the progress of our slow suicide. *Individual Christians* can determine to live responsibly in the environment regardless of the cost, knowing that a few well-placed examples can have a tremendous impact. We who have trusted in Christ have a rationale for ecological responsibility—we are demonstrating a fifth witness that God is reclaiming his world and bringing it new life.

On this point, Ralph Moerlling made a telling comment

a number of years ago: "If personal sacrifice is necessary to reclaim the earth, if we are compelled to give up luxuries and conveniences to which we have become accustomed, we can find our inspiration in the sign of the cross."[6] Jesus Christ left the glory of a place beside his Father to enter poverty and embrace death for the salvation of mankind. If we are to walk as he walked, surely part of our goal is to make the sacrifices necessary to image God in the earth.

Where would such sacrifices lead? Most ecologists agree that what is required is the so-called *sustainable ecosystem*, which may be defined as "one which has sufficient balance between living systems and sufficient stability to allow the ecosystem to continue long-term existence in spite of occasional disturbances."[7] We neither add to nor take from the ecosystem anything that would so alter its equilibrium that its ongoing life would be in danger.

In practical terms, the sacrificial life will mean buying fewer luxury goods, living in smaller and more energy-efficient homes, eating foods that are as unprocessed as possible, cooperating with government measures to decrease pollution and increase recycling, and working to put as much into the earth as we take out of it. This is a total reorientation of the North American dream. And we, because of Christ's call on our lives, have the privilege of serving as models to our society to show the way it could work.

GETTING INVOLVED

Assuming that we have made a decision to stand on the side of the fifth witness and make it work, where do we start? How can we begin demonstrating that God has laid claim to the world man is destroying by sin and pollution? Are there any concrete steps we can take? Let us consider several.

Educate Yourself

A large part of our inertia, even if we have a basic commitment to the environment, is a lack of clear information. Yet ecological self-education, in this era of awareness, is not difficult. Even regular viewing of television news and public affairs programming can work wonders.

Perhaps the best place to begin a self-education process, once you have exhausted the media in your own home, is your local public library. Books are easily accessible through subject headings such as "ecology" and "human ecology." A number of popular magazines regularly carry ecological information: *Time, Newsweek, Omni, Scientific American, Sierra,* and so on.

Determine to spend some time digging. Take notes, make photocopies, ask your friendly librarian for the latest information. You will be amazed at how much you can learn in a short time.

Clean Up Your Own Space

It appears biblically that we are most responsible for the circumstances of our immediate environment. Consider the parable of the Good Samaritan. As long as the priest and Levite were unaware of the wounded man, they had no responsibility for him. But the moment their eyes fell upon him, the moment they entered his space, they were under obligation to do something. In the same way, ecological responsibility must begin at home, with the things we touch and use. Here are some ideas of what you can do (you'll find a more complete list in the appendix):

• Check out the products you use at home. Are your aerosols propelled by chlorofluorocarbons that damage the ozone layer? Are the chemicals you use on your lawn and garden dangerous to the soil or to your neighbors?

(Keeping your lawn height at two to three inches and using lime can preclude the need for weed-killers). Are the materials you put in the trash potential ecological hazards? For example, could you do without disposable diapers (often labeled "ecological time bombs") or non-biodegradable plastic bags that will not decompose for five hundred years? Is there too much packaging on your food?

• Determine to live more simply. The accumulation of goods contributes to pollution probably more than any other factor. For every product you can do without, you have eased the burden on nature. Here it is easy to be cynical—if I don't buy it, someone else will. But we must recognize two things: First, we are not responsible for that "someone else," only for ourselves. Second, the actions of individuals, given enough individuals who begin living the same way, can have a powerful effect. Imagine if all the Christians in North America adopted a simpler lifestyle. Everyone would begin noticing the results. Don't worry about our growth economy collapsing because you are consuming less. It can stand to slow down somewhat anyway. If in time our change in buying patterns produces a different sort of economy, the outcome will be well worth the trauma getting there.

• Consider the power of recycling. Once considered a hobby horse of eccentrics, recycling has truly come into its own. Most major cities in North America have programs in place. Seattle, Washington, for example, supplies all trash containers for its residents and then charges extra fees for those who fill a second container of garbage in any one week. Recycled articles, however, are collected free of charge. A number of cities now provide specialized recycling containers for their residents and have designated trucks to pick up recycled goods. If your area does not have such a program, push for one. Not only will you help spare the environment a great deal of harmful garbage, but you will help slow the depletion of our natural resources.[8]

• Support the efforts of your government to turn the environmental crisis around. I am saddened at the thought of how many Christians continue to use leaded gas only because it is cheaper, or those who would rather die than spend time sorting garbage for recycling even when local bylaws demand it. We need to take seriously every environmental program available to us, whether legislated or voluntary. Our leaders are waking up to the dangers facing the earth, and the encouraging new laws in many of our communities need to be both applauded and supported.[9]

MAKE A STATEMENT

The goal of being a champion of the fifth witness is not merely to avoid damaging the earth. The fifth witness is based solidly in theology, in the statement that Christ has brought new life and that we are determined to image him properly as we declare his reclamation of what was lost in the Fall. We need to become both defenders of the earth and gardeners, enhancing its testimony to the glory and nurture of the Creator.

We must begin by assessing the possible role we could play in making a positive statement that the fifth witness is alive. For some Christians this role will be relatively large. Christian farmers, for example, have a good opportunity to reassess their intensive farming methods. Is there a better way to work the soil so that it is not damaged by pesticides and eroded by over-cultivation? Could the farm operated by a Christian stand out from its neighbors in the way it demonstrates that good land, nourished primarily by natural fertilizers and God's sun and rain, can produce more bountifully than land worked to death by greed?[10]

Those Christians involved in industries with the potential to pollute the environment may have a different role, one demanding a special kind of courage. In this case, making a statement about the fifth witness may involve assessing the pollution levels now produced by one's industry and suggesting modifications. It may even involve refusing to perform polluting work forbidden by law, taking a stand which may risk one's job but which is necessary if a Christian testimony is to be maintained.

Other believers may find a role in their communities—working for better recycling programs, calling for better environmental legislation, pointing out abuses. In all of this, we must make it clear that we are involved because the earth is the Lord's and he has renewed his claim to it by sending Christ to die for us and rise as ruler of his kingdom. We, therefore, are placing ourselves on God's side in defending nature against unwarranted damage.

For those with houses and yards, a strong statement will be made simply by beautifying the small portion of nature under our control. Plant flowers and trees. Make your yard shine for the glory of God. Declare through your personal environment that you are obeying God's original mandate to image him in your own space.[11] Even apartment dwellers can buy plants and make them flourish.

For those Christians whose potential impact on nature seems minimal, there are still ways we can incorporate the fifth witness into our testimony of the gospel. If society is buzzing with news of the latest ecological disaster, we can join the conversation by explaining why *we* are angry: We are angry not merely because the earth is a nice place to live and should not be damaged. We are angry because

God made the earth and owns it. He has set human beings in it to care for it. Since Christ has restored our broken relationship with the Father, we want to take up the task God has left us—to care for the earth he created and thus to declare that he has reclaimed it by sending his Son.

As we boldly include ecology in our statement of the gospel, we are showing that Christ is relevant to humanity's deepest needs. As well, we are opening the door to a new opportunity to introduce Christ to a world blindly on its way to uncreation.

Notes

1. David Douglas, "Wild Country and Wildlife: A Spiritual Preserve," *Christian Century*, 4-11 January 1984, 12.

2. William Dyrness, "Stewardship of the Earth in the Old Testament," *Tending the Garden: Essays on the Gospel and the Earth*, ed. Wesley Granberg-Michaelson (Grand Rapids: Wm. B. Eerdmans Publishing Co., 1987), 63.

3. Walter Houston, " 'And Let Them Have Dominion . . .': Biblical Views of Man in Relation to the Environmental Crisis," *Studia Biblica 1978: I*, ed. E. A. Livingstone (Sheffield, Eng.: JSOT Press, 1979), 178.

4. Robert P. Meye, "Invitation to Wonder: Toward a Theology of Nature," *Tending the Garden*, 47.

5. See Rene Dubos, "Franciscan Conservation versus Benedictine Stewardship," *Ecology and Religion in History*, ed. David and Eileen Spring (New York: Harper & Row, 1974), 124-26.

6. Ralph L. Moerlling, "Environmental Crisis and Christian Responsibility," *Concordia Theological Monthly*, 42 (March 1971): 181.

7. Donald R. Geiger, "Agriculture, Stewardship, and a Sustainable Future," *The Earth Is the Lord's: Essays on Stewardship*, ed. Mary Evelyn Jegen and Bruno Manno (New York: Paulist Press, 1978), 94-95.

8. The Mennonite Central Committee has begun a strong involvement in recycling programs, for which their main purpose is not to make money but to address environmental problems created by waste.

9. For example, Denver has legislated cleaner automobile fuels and has placed curbs on wood and coal burning. Voluntary "no-drive" days are encouraged (see Tom Graf, "Front Rangers Breathe Easier," *Sierra*, March/April 1988, 27-28). Los Angeles is planning impressive measures

to clean up its air pollution (see Philip Elmer-DeWitt, "A Drastic Plan to Banish Smog," *Time*, 27 March 1989, 49).

10. For several good suggestions see LaVonne Godwin Platt, *Hope for the Family Farm: Trust God and Care for the Land* (Newton, Kans.: Faith and Life Press, 1987).

11. Some ecologists, influenced by pantheism, have argued that gardening is just another example of western man's desire to control the earth. It is strange, however, that Japan, under strong influence from pantheistic religions, has developed gardening methods which far surpass the West in reshaping plants and trees to become something they never were by nature.

Christians in their gardens do need to be warned that it is God who gives the increase. We only plant and water. Whatever statement is made should reflect God's glory, not our own.

9

Propositions for a Christian Ecology

This is my Father's world,
And to my list'ning ears
All nature sings, and round me rings
The music of the spheres.
This is my Father's world!
I rest me in the thought
Of rocks and trees, of skies and seas—
His hand the wonders wrought.

This is my Father's world—
O let me ne'er forget
That though the wrong seems oft so strong
God is the Ruler yet.
This is my Father's world!
The battle is not done;
Jesus who died shall be satisfied,
And earth and heav'n be one.

If we have gained anything through our study of ecology in the light of Scripture, it must be to understand that the physical world is not irrelevant to the biblical Christian. The issue of the environment is fundamentally theological and is related to central truths of the Christian faith: creation, sin, salvation, and the proclamation of the gospel.

As we have studied the issues involved, we have discovered certain scriptural concepts that I hope have begun to transform our attitude to the world around us. Let us now consider a number of key propositions that will summarize our discoveries and point us to a biblical framework for dealing with the environmental crisis.

PROPOSITION ONE: *The earth is the Lord's.*

According to Psalm 24:1-2, the One who made the earth has claimed it for his own. All created things belong to him, and human beings can lay no claim to any part of the earth to exercise exclusive rights in exploiting its resources.

It is important that Christians affirm that ours is a *created* universe, formed by the God who owns it, for without this truth we become a law to ourselves. Such autonomy provides the recipe for ecological disaster. Only when we see ourselves as standing at the throne of God so that we can act under his orders do we have any hope of living responsibly in the environment.

PROPOSITION TWO: *Creation by nature speaks with two testimonies I have labeled the "bright witnesses"—glory and nurture.*

Both of these testify to and honor the Creator God, the first by showing his majesty through the complexity and beauty of what he has made, and the second by demonstrating that God intends to support abundantly the ongoing life he has created.

PROPOSITION THREE: *God has given mankind only one mandate concerning human interaction with the earth—to work the garden as his envoys on earth (Genesis 2:15).*

Our goal as people made by God is to nurture the environment, not to harm it; to support it, not to destroy it. Any notion of man's dominion over nature (a genuine biblical concept) must be tempered by two interwoven considerations. First, God created human beings to operate under his lordship; second, God intended mankind to "image" him in the earth, dealing with the environment as representatives of the Maker, as if he himself were at work.

PROPOSITION FOUR: *The human role of imaging God by working the Garden has as its desired end the enhancement of the bright witnesses.*

There was always a divine intention in mankind's tending of the earth. Just as all creation was to live in praise to its Creator, so human work in the physical world was intended to cause the bright witnesses to shine ever brighter and to testify ever louder to the God who made all that exists. Our mandate is to help creation shout the glory of God and exult in his power to nurture the life he formed.

PROPOSITION FIVE: *The physical creation serves as a mirror of the condition of the human heart, a tangible statement of an intangible reality.*

Human beings need concrete reminders of who they are before God. Thus the earth was created as a vast mirror of the human experience. In the Garden, the environment said to Adam and Eve, "You are the cherished higher creation of the God whose majesty you see around you. All that you require for life and happiness is easily within your grasp." By contrast, we must expect that rebellion against God in the spiritual realm would bring a corresponding harshness to the environment. Such was indeed the case.

PROPOSITION SIX: *In the face of the sin of mankind, two dark witnesses have been added to nature's proclamation—penalty and precariousness.*

These mirror images of the inner life of post-Fall humanity exist as opposites to the original bright witnesses. Instead of glory, we find condemnation in the mortality of all things, the horrors of natural disasters, and the growing crisis of ecological pollution. This is the witness of penalty. Instead of nurture, we discover that the earth no longer supports life without extreme effort, and that death can snuff out in an instant all that we have worked for. This is precariousness.

PROPOSITION SEVEN: *The four witnesses exist in a complex relationship with one another.*

The bright witnesses have not been eliminated by the dark ones but co-exist with them in a strange and (to us) uneasy relationship. At times, we still see the glory and nurturing power of the God who formed all that is and continues to allow it to survive. At other times, we are attacked by the dark witnesses which announce to us that human sinfulness can lead only to disaster.

PROPOSITION EIGHT: *Even after the Fall, God intended human beings to carry out the original mandate to care for the earth.*

Just because the first couple was driven from the Garden did not mean their responsibility to the earth had vanished. In the Scriptures there are many indications that the role of imaging (representing) God in the earth still remained his command to those who followed his ways. This is seen particularly through his instructions to the Israelites regarding their care of agricultural land, and through the many references to his continued rejoicing even over a fallen created order.

PROPOSITION NINE: *In seeming contradiction to his purposes, however, God in certain circumstances attacks his earth by becoming the Agent of the dark witnesses.*

He allows natural disasters to come upon apparently innocent people and refrains from preventing ecological disasters which occur with increasing frequency. But there is no contradiction in the Creator's actions. If humanity will not turn to him because of the testimony of the bright witnesses, then he brings the dark ones into play, not to destroy us but to call us to repentance and salvation.

PROPOSITION TEN: *Ultimately, the process of uncreation, whose first signs were observed as early as the Flood, will consume the earth and lead to a new creation.*

Our physical world truly is doomed, for all that is touched by sin must normally die and be reborn. We know, from 2 Peter 3:10-13 and Revelation 21:1-4, that this world will not be renewed but will one day be burned up utterly so that God can recreate it as a perfect world, the New Jerusalem where the Maker will dwell with his people. This, in itself, is not a motivation either for despair or for our own selfish exploitation of our environment. The command to work the existing Garden still stands, and there is much that can be done if we act from the proper perspective.

PROPOSITION ELEVEN: *We must understand that the ecological crisis arises from the sinfulness of the human heart; pollution* *enhances the dark witnesses and diminishes the testimony of the bright ones.*

To pollute deliberately or through carelessness is to make a statement about the condition of one's inner being, for the earth mirrors our hearts. Polluters assume falsely that the earth belongs to man, that greed is good, that economic advancement is the only true goal of humanity, and that sinful human beings can solve their own environmental problems. This complex of self-induced lies is symptomatic of hearts that are in rebellion against the One who made all things.

PROPOSITION TWELVE: *Because pollution is a reflection of sin, it is relevant to Christian experience and must be actively repudiated by all faithful believers.*

All of us pollute, and a basic amount of pollution is inevitable. But when we see the earth being destroyed because human beings do not feel it important to discover alternatives to ecological destruction, we no longer stand on neutral ground. This issue cannot be treated as if it were some lighthearted debate over whether it is better to have peanut butter or jam on your toast for breakfast. Ecological exploitation must be resisted strongly by believers because the earth is the Lord's and human support of the dark witnesses is wrong.

PROPOSITION THIRTEEN: *In the salvation won for us by Christ, we discover the potential for a fifth witness—reclamation—in which we can have an active part.*

When God sent his Son to earth to redeem us, he declared unequivocally his claim over human beings. If the earth reflects the condition of the human heart, then there is potential for a fifth witness by which Christians can allow the earth to demonstrate that God is reclaiming all things in Christ. As the Maker has taken hold of the lives of those committed to Christ, giving them new life, so too we can demonstrate, through environmental action, that God is laying claim as well to the world he made. As God's people, we intend to restore the earth to our Master's original plan for it.

PROPOSITION FOURTEEN: *The fifth witness involves not just the battle against the dark witnesses but support of the bright ones.*

We must by all means resist the scourge of pollution in the world. But the fifth witness does more—it strives to cause the earth to shine with the glory and nurture of God.

PROPOSITION FIFTEEN: *Under the mandate of the fifth witness, believers work in the earth through the power of the image of Christ, reborn in our hearts through salvation.*

Jesus lived the simple life, though he deserved the splendor of heaven. He sacrificed all, even his very survival, to obey his Father and win our salvation. To image God with the image of Christ is to live in contradiction with a world that scorns self-sacrifice and simplicity. We must be active, as followers of Christ's lifestyle, to so do our work in the earth that the earth itself will testify that God has reclaimed all things for himself, including both the souls of lost human beings and the environment in which they live.

It is important, as well, that we recapture the Bible's descriptions of God rejoicing in the creation he formed. The earth, despite the dark witnesses, is a place of beauty and grandeur. To be blind to that reality is to be blind to a crucial aspect of the work of God, for he did not merely create human beings—he gave them a stunning environment.

We need to begin to look at our world through the eyes of God to see what is fitting and what is not as we deal with the physical earth around us. As champions of the fifth witness, we must make it our goal to bring a certain kind of beauty to our surroundings, a beauty which harmonizes with nature rather than clashing with it. An example may elucidate the principle involved.

Only this morning, my son Shawn and I went for a hike in the hills above my parents' home in the interior of British Columbia. These hills are uninhabited but show definite signs of human activity—portions of them have been logged, and there are dirt roads wandering everywhere. Yet there is a harmonious beauty there which reflects the goal of champions of the fifth witness. The logging was done judiciously so that, over the years, intriguing meadows have formed and many new trees, though small, have sprung up. The roads are unobtrusive and serve more to lead the hiker deeper into the wilderness than to jar him with ugliness.

Yet, near the edge of a small lake, we came upon a 1972 Toyota, wheels to the sky. It had obviously been driven to death (the oil pan was punctured in two places), then rolled down the embankment. All of the windows had been smashed and two of the tires removed.

It was an ugly sight. Why? Partly because it spoke of a gratuitous waste of the earth's resources—the metal and other materials required to produce lt. But my main objection was that it did not belong there. In a vehicle scrapyard, it would not have attacked my senses, but in the wilderness it spoke of human beings who had no sense of place, no inkling that they had defiled a testimony to the Maker of these hills.

There is a difference between harmonious beauty where, even though touched by man, creation flourishes in witness to God, and ugliness—the ignorant abuse of the earth, as offensive as someone stomping on your new carpet with muddy boots. The difference lies in the degree to which actions in the environment reveal an innate sense of awe for the One who made it.

Clear-cut logging, despite the arguments that it is the only economical way to do the job, is ugly; well-tended farms are beautiful. An oil spill is an obscene blot; a carefully planned garden is a delight. A vacant lot full of discarded fast food containers is a disgrace; a replanted young forest is a place of wonder. All reflect the controlling hand of human beings. Yet beauty shines when God's handiwork, though modified, is allowed to demonstrate the majesty of the Maker rather than the achievements of man.

If we are to announce to the world that God has reclaimed it in Christ, we need to capture for ourselves a sense of what it means for our battered earth again to proclaim his glory. Thus we must make proper distinctions between what exhibits harmonious beauty (though the beauty may often be less than pristine) and what jars us with its greedy, careless disregard for the purposes of God in nature.

Through our efforts, we must allow creation to shine for God, to be different from what it is now in its reflection of the darkness of the human heart. We must rejoice in the earth so that it may rejoice in turn and proclaim that God is still its ruler.

As Twentieth Century Christians, we live in an uncomfortable tension. On the one hand, we know that the earth and its lost inhabitants are doomed, no matter how many reforms are encouraged or legislated. On the other hand, we are called to present a gospel message, to reach, by any legitimate means, at least some of those who would other-wise go to a terrible eternity.

If it is possible to make care for the earth part of our witness, then we must get involved in the environment. We know that creation will one day be destroyed. But if we can, even for a few moments, cause it to flower in honor of the One who made it and has reclaimed it, then its ulti-mate destiny will be far less tragic.

No new day can begin without having a night to pre-cede it. We contemplate the earth at sunset. Now is the time to make it blaze with glory just once more, before the night falls and a new day shines.

Getting Involved Where You Are

*Thirty-nine environmental tips for the householder
and eleven more for churches*

The following insights are not particularly profound. Some of them may not work in your situation. But they are a start toward a new attitude toward your role as one of the planet's polluters. Any public library can provide you with further information to take you beyond this basic list.

ENVIRONMENTAL TIPS FOR THE HOUSEHOLDER

Recycling

1. *Recycle whatever you can*: bottles, cans, newspapers, cardboard, plastic. Not only will you cut down on the volume going into the garbage dump, but you will help to slow the depletion of natural resources needed to produce new products.

2. *Reuse materials you would otherwise throw out.* Christmas cards can be cut up for decorative displays or gift labels;

torn clothes can become cleaning rags; plastic containers can hold other products.

3. *Recycle old toys, furniture, clothing, and other household items through thrift shops, garage sales, and so on.*

Garbage

4. *Establish a "banned" list for items that must never go into the garbage*: containers with poison or corrosive indicators on them, alkaline batteries, paint cans. Call a local environmental agency to get the address of the nearest toxic waste dump, and deposit these things there.

5. *Use cloth diapers or a diaper service rather than disposables.*

6. *Become a composter.* Your local library can provide you with information on the construction of a compost box. You will be amazed at how much wet garbage you can turn into good soil.

7. *Work hard at reducing your volume of garbage.*

Your Home

8. *Conserve energy as much as possible.* Turn out lights, turn down your furnace or air conditioner, check your insulation and sources of heat/coolness loss, put full loads into your washer and dryer, and so on. The less energy you burn, the less you are supporting the pollution which results from producing it.

9. *Reconsider the type of home heating fuel you use.* Natural gas and propane burn far cleaner than oil and wood (though the newer wood furnaces are much less polluting than older varieties).

10. *Have your home furnace serviced regularly so that it burns efficiently.*

11. *Buy a water-saving shower head.* It will soon pay for

itself by conserving water as well as the energy needed to heat the water.

12. *Turn down the thermostat on your hot water heater to 125 degrees Fahrenheit.*

13. *Insulate your hot water heater.* It will waste less energy. Kits are available at your local building supply dealer.

14. *Put a quart-sized sealed plastic bottle full of water in your toilet tank.* Every flush will save a quart of water, and your toilet will still function well.

Your Yard

15. *Consider cutting down on the amount of lawn in your yard and substituting flowers, shrubs and trees.* Lawns require potentially damaging fertilizers, and lawn clippings often end up choking garbage dumps.

16. *Consider using a manual, non-motorized lawn mower.* It is good exercise and your neighbors will appreciate the quiet. If your mower has a motor, keep it running efficiently. Blue smoke is a bad sign.

17. *Avoid chemical fertilizers and pesticides for your yard.* There are safer natural products available. Contact your local nursery or environmental agency.

18. *Compost your leaves and lawn clippings.* If you can locate the proper machine, shred your tree clippings and use the mulch.

Your Car

19. *Drive less.* Walk and cycle more. Use public transportation whenever you can.

20. *If your engine has to idle more than thirty seconds, turn it off.* Your car should not need to warm up more than one minute, even on a cold day.

21. *Keep your car well maintained.* It will run better and more cheaply, and it will pollute less.

22. *If you are changing your own oil in your car, buy recycled oil.* It works just as well as new oil and preserves natural resources. Urge your service station to provide recycled oil as an option.

23. *Waste products from your car (old oil, antifreeze, batteries, tires) are all dangerous to the environment. Contact your environmental agency for disposal instructions.* Be aware that some antifreezes can kill dogs and cats which are attracted by the taste.

24. *When you replace your car, stress low gas mileage and sophisticated pollution controls as requirements.*

Purchases

25. *Avoid groceries with excessive non-recyclable packaging.* All that wrapping will end up in your local landfill site. Watch out for the recent spawning of microwaveable products, usually wrapped in lots of plastic.

26. *When possible, buy products packaged in glass rather than plastic containers, and then recycle the glass.* In general, choose packaging that is easily recyclable.

27. *Purchase organically grown produce.* This will help the movement to eliminate the use of damaging environmental products in agriculture. The reason organic produce is so expensive is that not enough is sold. Yet the majority of people who are surveyed say they prefer foods grown without chemicals.

28. *Use biodegradable, phosphate-free cleaning products*: dishwashing soaps, laundry detergents, and so on. Phosphates promote algae growth which damages waterways.

30. *Buy toilet paper made from recycled, nonbleached fibers.*

31. *Stop using disposable paper towels, in favor of reusable varieties.*

32. *Do not buy disposable plastic or foam products*: dishes, cups, utensils, razors, cameras, and so on.

33. *Reconsider your use of plastic shopping bags.* Ask for paper ones or invest in reusable cloth bags, such as some supermarkets are now selling. If you do use plastic bags, shop at a store which recycles them; don't use them for your garbage.

34. *When buying an appliance, stress energy efficiency.*

35. *Buy only the appliances you need.* Every product produced has added to pollution in the world and has depleted natural resources.

36. *Buy used items when you can:* tools, appliances, automobiles, even clothing. Every item used by more than one owner has saved the earth some degree of damage required to produce a new one. But be careful that your used gadget does not sacrifice energy efficiency.

37. *When you purchase new products, go for good quality and plan to keep what you own rather than joining the throw-away society.*

38. *Choose rechargeable batteries over alkaline ones.* It will cost you less in the long run, and every recharge is, in effect, a recycling.

39. *Change your attitude.* Go over the material in chapter 8 and begin getting a feel for the kind of mind-set that both uses less and wastes less. See yourself for who you are: a polluter who must be determined to pollute God's earth as little as possible and take no more from it than you put back in.

ENVIRONMENTAL TIPS FOR CHURCHES

40. *Plan for greater energy efficiency in your building.* Insulate, use energy efficient equipment, and so on.

41. If *possible, install separate heating/cooling thermostats for each area of your building.* That way, you need control only the climate of the area you are using.

42. *Install timers on your light and climate controls.*

43. *Use your building more for community organizations.* Not only will you reach out to your community better, but you will save these groups from having to use energy elsewhere. In general, most church buildings are terribly under-utilized for the natural resources used to produce them and the energy required to power them.

44. *Apply tip 15 above to your grounds.*

45. *Check with your photocopier company regarding the dangers of waste toner.* If there is hazard to the environment, dispose of it at a toxic waste site.

46. *Seek ways to reduce the amount of trash produced out of your building.* Can some things be reused or recycled? For example, it may be possible to recycle old office paper.

47. *Try to locate sources of recycled paper for your copier and office supplies.*

48. *Cut down on junk mail by asking suppliers to stop sending it.* If they refuse, send it back to them at their expense. Useless mail uses up resources and fills garbage dumps needlessly.

49. *Assess your church's use of disposable cups and dishes.* Perhaps your regular members could set up a "bring a mug" program for Sunday morning coffee (with a few spares for visitors).

50. *Make care for the environment the spiritual issue it should be.* If the church will lead the way, believers will be more likely to change their own attitudes and behavior.

Scripture Index

Subject Index